Dear Lovi—
May God bless you
in every way...
on every day...
for always

A Son's HANDBOOK

Bringing Up Mom with Alzheimer's/Dementia

Stephen W. Hoag, Ph.D.

Inspiring Voices®

A Service of **Guideposts**

Inspiring Voices books may be ordered through booksellers or by contacting:

Inspiring Voices
1663 Liberty Drive
Bloomington, IN 47403
www.inspiringvoices.com
1 (866) 697-5313

ISBN: 978-1-4624-0841-2 (sc)
ISBN: 978-1-4624-0842-9 (e)

Library of Congress Control Number: 2013921854

Printed in the United States of America.

Inspiring Voices rev. date: 01/07/2014

This book is dedicated to my mother,
Bertha E. Hoag.

Contents

Acknowledgments

There are many people who touched our lives during Mom's lifetime who directly, indirectly, or inadvertently made the events of the last ten years of Mom's life just a little better.

To my loving wife, Gina, thank you for all the late nights, early mornings, and "Bert Alerts" that we shared with Mom. To my daughters, Maureen and Kathleen, thanks for always saying yes when we needed you.

There are not enough appropriate words of appreciation to describe the encouragement of Patrick Saty, the first to demand that I write so others might be helped.

In the final years of Mom's life, there were many doctors who cared for her while allowing her to express herself in song and dance in their respective places of service. We especially wish to express our appreciation to Dr. Richard Wein, Dr. Gary Tansino, and Dr. Robert Biondino.

Special expression of love to Tommy, my brother, who worked through his own struggles during Mom's last ten years. He was always there doing everything he could to love and care for our mother.

To my loving colleagues June, Lori, Judy, Diane, Lee, Harold, Harriet, and Charlene, who often witnessed my dashes for the door to get to Mom's side; heard my pleadings on the telephone in conversations with mother; and saw the tears in my eyes that I tried so hard to hide, God bless you.

It the final few years of Mom's life we needed the assistance of a woman of strength, character, and compassion to meet the mounting challenges of Mother's declining condition. Chelsea Schultz was part of many moments articulated in this book, but most importantly, someone who always gave unselfishly of herself to Mom, my brother, and our entire family.

Introduction

Not in the Son's Handbook

As with all things regarding Mom, there was music. The anecdotes, stories, and lessons learned and contained in these pages would best make Mom happy if put to music, and in some fashion, they have been.

My mother was born Bertha Ethel Bever on December 23, 1914, in Fitchburg, Massachusetts, the second youngest of eight sisters and one older brother. She was known by her friends and family as Bokie or Bert. To me, she was just Mom.

I am Stephen (Stevie, as Mom called me), the younger of Bertha's two sons. Tommy, Bertha's oldest son and my brother, is a quiet, honest guy who is mentally retarded and often emotionally fragile. Joe, Bertha's husband of fifty-two years and my father, was a difficult man to cope with and understand. Dad was often intimidating and violent and, like Mom very musically talented.

When I was a child, my mom was my best friend, teacher, and confidant. As I stepped out of our home and into the world to achieve some victories and absorb some failures, Mom and I grew distant, as some parents and children do.

When Dad died, Mom and Tommy became my responsibility. In the cyclical fashion of life, Mom was mine to love and care for, almost as she had done for me as a young boy. You see, Mom lived the last dozen years of her life with Alzheimer's disease/dementia, and I shared the last ten years meeting the challenges of this disease with her.

Despite the endless string of pamphlets, medical journals, websites, and bookstore offerings, there was no handbook for sons on how to take care of a mother with Alzheimer's/dementia. Generally speaking, there is no how-to or operations manual for sons in general. There are how-to books on gardening, home repairs, hitting a baseball, and for virtually every topic one can name. How is it no one has written one on being a son of someone dealing with this disease?

However, there is an *implied* how-to manual for sons. Although not written down anywhere, it is the fusion of all the rules and routines that parents impart to us. Generally included are such standards as brushing your teeth, washing your face and hands, kissing your aunt, shaking your uncle's hand, not fighting with your brother, doing all your homework, taking out the trash, and walking the dog. But nowhere in that implied son's handbook is there a chapter on what to do when your mother or father is stricken with Alzheimer's disease/dementia, and you as the son must take care of him or her.

This narrative represents the synthesis of ten years and thousands of pages of a daily chronicle I wrote when Mom became the most important responsibility in my life. With great prayer, my writing allowed me to navigate the mental, emotional, and physical challenges of this disease on my mother and me. These brief chapters offer no clinical or medical advice. That remains the domain of trained medical professionals. Rather, this narrative focuses on common issues relative to Alzheimer's/dementia that we as sons and daughters are compelled to address every moment of every day, armed with nothing more than what our parents and God have given us: our love.

With each entry, I asked God to impart a lesson to me. With the tug on my heart and the greater damage dementia brought to my mother, I needed to learn how to meet all her needs. To be sure, I didn't care for my mother alone, but sitting in the decision-making chair was just me. Each day during a quiet moment I wrote down what I saw, how I responded, and what worked and what didn't. I sure made a lot of mistakes. Many evenings I sat at Mom's beside with my pad on my lap and wrote every word she uttered. I recorded her expressions and my feelings as clearly as I could. My chronicle sometimes looked like an exercise in the Cornell note-taking system because I wanted to be a better son, a better man than I was.

With my "suddenly" moment with Mother regarding the first salvo of Alzheimer's/dementia against my limited frame of reference, I realized I wasn't prepared. The reality that I was inadequate to correctly address Mom's uncontrollable bodily functions, dramatic mood swings, and fantasy melodramas mixed with the basics of her daily care sometimes overwhelmed me. The only constant and bastion of strength was my knowing that God had this whole situation in control. I was exactly where God wanted me, doing precisely what He required me to do. My daily writing was my way of connecting all the pieces of my life that were changed due to Mother's Alzheimer's/dementia.

At the end of most chapters is a "Son's Rule." Each represents a lesson I learned that day so I might approach the next hour or the next dementia-generated challenge as a better son. God is always talking to us, especially in times of great tribulation, and He uses an endless number of methods and vehicles by which to communicate with and teach us all we need to know to meet the imminent task. I wasn't good enough to take care of my mother alone, and I knew it. But by the grace of God; my loving wife, Gina; my incredible daughters Maureen and Kathleen; my brother, Tommy; Companions & Homemakers, the Connecticut Agency on Aging; and Chelsea Schultz, Mom and I put on a great performance.

Chapter 1

Suddenly

With each passing day we seem to be confronted with a steady stream of "all-of-a-suddens." *All of a sudden* I slipped on the ice. *All of a sudden* the car came from out of nowhere. *All of a sudden* the cell phone went dead. *All of a sudden* I felt sick to my stomach. However, there is no more dramatic all-of-a-sudden moment than when you realize the care of a parent is all yours.

For me it occurred on June 23, 2002, when I went to the hospital to see my father, who only one day earlier had been diagnosed with lung cancer. Upon my arrival, the nurse met me at the door to his room and told me he didn't have long to live. Less than an hour later, Dad died in my arms as I tried to speak to him.

My emotions were convoluted and muted only by momentary tears as I realized in that moment that the total care of my eighty-seven-year-old mother and retarded brother now fell on me. When I told my daughters that their grandfather had died, Kathleen, in her inimitable manner, suggested my life had just changed forever (see Chapter 3, "Life as You Know It"). She was correct in so many ways. I suddenly viewed my professional life through a new lens, as my priorities had been placed in a metaphorical sack, shaken up, and poured out into a new order on the ground before me. As I would discover in those ten years of days and nights with Mom on our long road with Alzheimer's/dementia, the "suddenlys" became much more a momentary thing.

As a rather well-organized and pragmatic man, chaos is not a welcomed partner. I couldn't defend against the unknown manifestations of dementia and the speed with which it took a little part of Mom, day by day. I couldn't prepare for the instantaneous change in Mom's needs due to the rapid fire "suddenlys" of hallucinations and volatile emotions, both hers and mine.

The events, moments, and lessons contained in these pages are those of a typical man who continues to live through the process of love. Indeed, it is a process because it is impossible to provide the extremes of care without leading with love. I am not an exceptional man in this regard, just one who believes with all my heart and soul that God will direct my walk and forgive me for the many missteps I have made in caring for Mom and my brother.

Matthew 6:21 states, "For where your treasure is, there your heart will be also." I did not seek nor did I want these responsibilities, but the treasure of your heart is the people who most need your love. It is a hard dichotomy to deal with each day, but loving family members who need our love is far more challenging than loving those who are in a position to give and take in balanced proportion.

As we all should learn, love is not an emotion. It is an act of will.

Chapter 2

Curtain Going Up: Alzheimer's/Dementia

In what was a portent of things to come, Mother had a heart attack and stroke in my arms in 1999. I was sitting at the kitchen table with Mom and Dad as they ate breakfast one morning. Suddenly, Mom's eyes developed a faraway gaze, and she dropped her spoon. After yelling, *"Mom!"* and receiving no reply, she started to keel over, and I caught her in my arms before she fell on the floor. I said to Dad, who was now standing and watching all of this, "Call 911!" Flabbergasted, Dad could not move. I screamed, *"Call 911!"* again and then grabbed the telephone off the kitchen table and dialed 911 myself while still holding my mom in my arms.

My father failed me in that moment, but the ambulance arrived in short order. On my knees in the ambulance next to her, I talked to Mom, begging her to not die on me. I immediately became scared when I remembered how riveted to the spot my father was and how Tommy just stared as the emergency technicians took Mom out the front door. Worried about them both, I felt so alone. I asked God to stand with me, and He did.

After that and Mom's subsequent quadruple-bypass surgery, I began feeling a greater sense of urgency and seriousness of purpose with every moment she and I spent together. Gone were the casual moments of "Hello, Mom" and the obligatory one-liners that followed, such as, "Hi, Mom, how old is the captain?" followed by her oft-repeated, well-rehearsed comeback of "Go ask him, he's on the poop deck," or "Hi, Mom, what's shakin'?" and my mother's response, "Uncle Henry's leg, when he pees."

The vaudevillian banter of those lighthearted times of my early youth when Mom taught me a hundred one-liners before I reached the age of ten quickly disappeared. I missed that part of our relationship and miss her and them still.

Before I knew dementia was creeping into her life, I recognized alterations in our relationship. The lightness of the past we once knew was replaced with focused caregiving and intense love-giving. My emotions of concern, empathy, and sometimes spurts of anger were draining.

I was given some important instruction by super professionals of the Connecticut Agency on Aging. They didn't waste a minute in their approach and had little patience with any "woe-is-me" emotionality by the family members of parents with Alzheimer's/dementia. As I came to understand their mission, and now mine, they tactfully taught me to stop thinking about how every situation affected me. The focus of time, task, and emotion had to be on Mom. That meant "check your feelings at the door and do what is required and do it in a timely manner." This probably was the most difficult of all challenges, at least early on.

Feeding Mom in the post-bypass surgery days was a breeze compared to the daily tasks that lay ahead as the dementia took a little bit more of her with each week. Despite my self-styled belief that I could somehow heal Mom from dementia (the symptom package for Alzheimer's) with dedication, hard work, and intellect, I soon learned to appreciate the magnitude of the tagline of Alzheimer's disease/dementia: *"First it takes your mind, and then it takes your body."*

Chapter 3

Life as You Know It Is Over

The dynamic of the relationship between mothers and sons is totally dissimilar from son to son or mother to mother. Throughout my youth and into my adult years, I was forever curious about how boys/men I knew interacted with their mothers. I think my curiosity stemmed from the fact that I was under the inclination that my mother and I had the most unique relationship of any mother and son on the planet.

My mother and father never used the words "I love you." During my boyhood years I heard other mothers telling their sons and daughters they loved them, and I often wondered why them and not me. When I was seven or eight, I asked my mother why she and Dad didn't say "I love you." All these years later I can remember her immediate answer: "Because we don't need to say it."

I never pursued a more definitive answer from Mother, and I sure wasn't asking Dad that question. However, with or without those three words, I loved my parents and am sure they loved me too, but I never lost my fascination with how sons and moms interacted.

When I became a teacher in Norristown, Pennsylvania, I got a kick out of parents' night because I got a chance to let the parents talk about their children. I asked them more questions than they asked me as their children's teacher.

Many years later when I was constructing the Developing Tomorrow's Professionals program, a groundbreaking endeavor for Black and Latino young men to prepare them to fully embrace the world of lifelong education, leading to graduation from college, we included specific activities for our young men with their mothers.

Whatever the relationship was between Mom and me prior to my father's death on June 23, 2002, it dramatically changed that day. For with my dad's sudden passing, all of the caretaking functions for my eighty-seven-year-old mother and older brother formerly performed by Dad fell to me.

I rather vividly remember the day he died, as most people who lose a parent do. My father had been hospitalized for what doctors diagnosed as a punctured lung in April 2002. He was moved to a rehabilitation facility, and I had hoped he would soon return home to my mother and brother. He wasn't there but a week when he fell in his room and was quickly returned to the hospital. This led to another lengthy stay.

I spent three to five hours a day with him during his two-month hospitalization and convalescence, and he was just as full of the ole blarney as ever. The day he fell, the doctors told me he didn't break anything but they were obliged to run some tests.

I was at the office in Hartford when Mid-State Medical called to tell me a doctor who I did not know wanted to talk to me about my dad's condition.

I scooted over there after work, whereupon this grim-faced physician informed me Dad had a fully metastasized cancer the size of his fist in his lung. (So much for the collapsed lung diagnosis.) He proceeded to explain that Dad had little time remaining and recommended I move him to hospice.

The recollections of my emotions at that moment are too convoluted to glean a single feature, but I know my first few thoughts were of my mother and brother.

I went directly from the hospital to my mother and brother's home, the house my parents had built and occupied since 1962. The drive from the hospital to 11 Woodland Drive was about twenty minutes, and I wondered exactly what I would

6

say to Mom and how I would have to speak to her in relative privacy so as not to excite my older brother, Tom, who is retarded and emotionally very fragile.

Mom had only recently showed some signs of absentmindedness and some disassociation between the past and the present. I assumed it was *just a matter of getting old.* I would soon find myself on the low end of the Alzheimer's disease learning curve.

Driving there I kept thinking about the relationship Dad and Mom had these past fifty-two years. There was love and companionship to be sure, but I never saw much affection or smiles between them. The one thing that kept going through my mind was that during the nine weeks Dad had been confined to a hospital or nursing care facility, Mom had only come to see him twice. She never said she missed him and was rather cavalier when I asked her each day if she wanted to go with me to hospital. She just said, "No, not today."

I was never surprised or disappointed. It was just Mom. She was never one to express love, except to my brother, who needed her in every way.

As I pulled into the driveway, I knew I had to be matter-of-fact with her. There would be no tears from Mom. This I knew. She once told me she no longer had any tears left for anyone, but this was her husband of more than a half century.

I walked in right around their dinnertime, and Mom was sitting at the kitchen table reading a magazine with the cat close at hand. I sat across from her at the little kitchen table and looked at her for a few minutes. As usual it was like I was invisible, but after a moment Mom said, "We're just about to have supper and you're sitting in Tommy's chair."

The relationship of mother and her number-two son was often beset with intrigue, disassociated parts of my youth and adulthood, her high expectations for me, and the disappointment I had been to her relative to the choice of a career. And there were the ever-present variations of drama.

Love, with all the literary machinations, is rarely written about as it relates to mother and son. I loved my mother as much or more than when I was a child, but Mom limited the opportunities to demonstrate my love—that is, until the day she died.

Now sitting across from her as I had many hundreds of times before, I had to tell her her husband had a few days to live. That reality hadn't even climbed into my heart yet, and here I was trying to select the words to go along with *terminal cancer ... hospice ... death.*

I asked Mom to put down the paper as I needed to talk with her about Dad. She ignored my request. I asked a second time, and she explained this is the time she and the cat, Sherbie, read the paper together.

Losing some patience and feeling pressured by the circumstances that Tommy was in the next room and listened to everything, I went around the small oval kitchen table to her side, knelt next to her, and spoke almost in a whisper in her ear. "Mom," I started, "I just came from the hospital. They're moving Dad to hospice tomorrow."

Mother did not react. In fact, she showed no response whatsoever. My faith is forever active in every type of circumstance and I believe God is sitting in the driver's seat in my life. God knows my heart's desire, but then I spoke out loud, "God, please help me now; guide my words." I did not want to be the cause of any type of pain to my mother, but this was one time in my life I could not avoid. There was no one left but me.

I slowly said in her left ear, "Mom, Dad has terminal cancer and only has maybe a few days to live."

Mom never broke from her paper. With the cat sitting on her lap, looking up at her, mom calmly said, "What are you worried about? Your father is getting better. He'll be home soon. Now leave me alone and let me read my paper. If you want to do something, go make me dinner."

I can't explain how inadequate I felt. I was as *useless* as my father sometimes accused me of being.

Leaving the house without a good-bye, I returned to the hospital, finding my father as I had left him the day before, unable to speak beyond a whisper, his face badly swollen. I talked to him and he looked at me. It wasn't a conversation, just me telling him I loved him, hoping maybe he would say he loved me. It didn't happen.

The next day was Sunday, and I went to see him first thing in the morning. I didn't stay long. He wasn't conscious, just sleeping quietly, having a little trouble breathing. There were so many thoughts going through my head. How long would he live? The doctor said a few months, maybe three. What should I do first when Dad dies? I was just beginning to deal with this reality and didn't have a single answer or a plan.

I wanted to get my head clear and have a conversation with God, so I decided to take a drive down Route 9 where the Connecticut countryside is at its most serene. I wasn't in the car more than twenty minutes when I knew I had to go back to the hospital and see my dad.

Arriving at the hospital, I went directly to my father's room, where I was met at the door by his nurse. She looked at me with this almost-in-tears look. She knew my name and said, "Stephen, your father doesn't have long."

I corrected her with the doctor's own words from yesterday when he'd said they were moving Dad to hospice tomorrow. She didn't say another word as I entered the room and heard my father grasping for breath. It is a sound I shall never forget, although I wish I could. His face was more swollen than the day before and a dark-orange color.

The nurse came to my side as I sat at bedside with my face a few inches from his. She asked me if I wanted them to try to revive him if he stops breathing. I looked at my dad and said, *"Dad?"* as if I really expected him to awaken and tell me what to do. I told the nurse no.

For the next twenty minutes I talked to him. I told him I would take care of Mom and Tommy. And I told him I loved him over and over.

Then I said, "Dad, please tell me you love me, just once." All at once the heavy breathing ended. I knew he was gone.

Once again, I was alone. I should have prayed for Mom and Tommy at that moment, but I prayed for me.

I was with Dad in that room for an hour. I sat close to him and prayed.

Before I left, I decided not to go directly to Mom and tell her Dad had died. I needed to remove my personal expectations of her reactions to the news of his death ... I could not judge her. I would not let myself judge her. I accepted that Mom may not or could not understand what really had happened. The early impact of Alzheimer's/dementia had first taken its toll on me. How was I to move forward with all I had to do now that Dad was dead if I couldn't begin with the basic task of telling Mom her husband had died?

I went home. My twin daughters were in the living room when I arrived.

I sat down and told them their grandfather was dead.

Maureen moved across the room, sat next to me, and said softly, "I'm sorry, Dad."

Kathleen looked at me from the couch and said matter-of-factly, "Dad, life as you know it is over."

Seven more dramatic and accurate words were never spoken.

Her words cut through me like a hot knife through butter.

Suddenly I knew all the responsibilities for the welfare and happiness of my mother and brother had just fallen right into my lap.

All my skills and compartmentalization of my professional and family duties would be now put to the test. My mother, Bertha, once a bastion of strength and direction was entering a period of diminishing mental and physical capabilities. My brother, Tom, who relied on my mother as his best friend, his strength, and his decision-maker would be pulled downward as our mother slowly lost her fight for her identity and eventually her life.

God stood with me in the gap during this troubled time. I was alone with God—no better partner during this time—but I was not prepared for the times to come.

No son (or daughter) could be prepared for a parent with Alzheimer's/dementia. There was no "son's book of rules" or "operations manual" of what to do. Alzheimer's/dementia was the enemy, and my love and faith in Christ Jesus was my armor, my shield, and my guiding force.

My love for Mom and Tommy was the driving force that motivated me to never quit on them, no matter what the state agencies and private organizations suggested was best.

Son's Rule: Do not accept, as an absolute, the recommendations of the organizations and individuals who seek what they believe is best for your mom or dad. Do not let fear wear you down. Remember, God never lets you meet any adversary *He* doesn't give you the tools and weapons to overcome. You are never alone. God is forever with you. His love, and yours for your father or mother, can never be defeated.

Chapter 4

The Beauty Parlor

Bordering on being one of the "little miracles of life," I experienced a much-needed blessing on the Saturday that followed my father's death. The suddenness of his passing on Monday, June 3, 2002, left the care of my mom, who was showing the initial phase of Alzheimer's/dementia, with me. During those first few days an endless number of responsibilities seemed to stack themselves up on my shoulders. I felt ill-equipped to meet all that was required of me, but my walk with God kept me reasonably balanced.

What weighed on my heart as a real distraction was that I was harboring some resentment toward Mom for refusing to be engaged in the last few months of Dad's life, comporting herself with a "what's all the fuss about" attitude. I had a lot to learn about Alzheimer's/dementia, but my heart was not immediately forgiving during those first few days that followed his death.

Praying to God to lift any resentment or negativity from my heart, I hoped my prayer would be answered expeditiously as the funeral as the entire cavalcade of post-life tasks were lining up before me. Never one to spend a great deal of time with my parents when Dad was alive, I now found myself doting all over Mom, from making her coffee to washing her clothes. I was trying to be everything all at once to her during her time of mourning.

The only problem was, she wasn't mourning. She didn't want to talk about funeral arrangements or phone calls I made to my father's brothers or bringing in extra food if anyone were to stop by. To Mom, all was business as usual, but that didn't stop me from fawning all over her, and she got annoyed with me quite often, asking me to go home and leave her alone.

One of the first things I did was schedule an appointment with her hairdresser—otherwise known as the "beauty parlor." Mom, like most of the women of her generation, would have periodic appointments at the beauty parlor. I had never gone with her to the beauty parlor and assumed it was like going to the barber to get a haircut. How wrong I was about this little piece of American heritage.

This one event changed how I looked at my mother for the rest of her life. This little miracle was exactly what I needed to see her with more loving eyes, a greater depth of understanding, and a far more sensitive approach to all that Alzheimer's/dementia would bring to bear.

On the morning of her beauty parlor appointment, I helped Mom down the stairs from her bedroom, and she looked so vibrant. She was actually rather giddy, and I could not understand why. Again, she still seemed oblivious to the fact that her husband had just passed away a few days ago. She was wearing more makeup than usual, and I complimented her on how good she looked.

I escorted her to the car, holding the door for her as always. She slowly turned, sat down on the passenger seat, and then swung her legs into place. That was Mom's unique way of getting into a car. She asked me to turn on the radio so she could hear "my kind of music." I knew the appropriate radio station for Mom. It was 88.5 on the dial, one focused on jazz, big bands, and singers of the 1940s and '50s.

I had never been to Mom's beauty parlor before, but I knew the streets of Wallingford rather well, so I had no problem finding the location. Upon our arrival, I was looking at a wooden building, a very old structure, but there was no sign of any kind that indicated that a hairdressing establishment was on the premises. Had this been two years or more in the future, I would have figured this location for an Alzheimer's/dementia illusion.

The building sat across the street from where W. T. Grants (a department store chain that operated some thirty years ago, when the world was a whole different place) used to be. We parked on the street and entered a small narrow door with no landing, just a straight up staircase of twelve stairs. The stairs were old, rickety, and had a single handrail, and Mom slowly ascended, stopping three times to catch her breath. I stood tight behind her, poised to catch her if she faltered, staying one step beneath the one she climbed.

Hearing voices from the door at the top of the stairs, Mom said, "That sounds like Mae."

Entering the cut-glass knobbed entrance, I was instantly transported to a hairdressing salon of 1957. The pictures on the walls were of models with 1950s hairstyles, most of them yellowing and dog-eared.

The room was tiny, maybe ten feet wide and fifteen feet long. The clients were all senior citizens, all well over the age of desirability. The chairs had drying hoods, even the one I sat on. Each of these chairs had obviously been covered, repaired, and/or reupholstered more than a few times in the last fifty years.

There were standup ashtrays. Mae, the matron/owner/stylist, had a 1961 bouffant hairstyle, was heavily made up, and stood poised with a cigarette between her fingers in perfect character.

As she hugged Mom upon her arrival with the words, "Bertha, darling," the ashes from her cigarette fell to the worn-out throw rug that was long a part of the stained tile floor.

The radio, an old Zenith, with horizontal tuning, was tuned to a station that played Wayne Newton, Ed Ames, and the "Alley Cat." Mom had taken a seat and proceeded to say hello to all five of the gum-chewing (or just gumming) clientele as they sat underneath loudly humming drying hoods with curlers and magazines.

I sat in a chair next to the door and intently watched Mom, but I tried not to listen too closely and make her uncomfortable. I know I had never looked at my mother quite the way I did that day. Mom began a conversation with a woman who was clearly *not* listening to anything Mom was saying. Mom was picking cat hairs off her slacks and explaining to the woman that she had a white-haired cat and how she could *not* be expected not to have cat hair on her (polyester) blue slacks. "After all," Mom said, "I love the cat."

The patrons all sat in their respective hooded chairs, appearing to be in a rather dazed state, thumbing through magazine pages and often snapping their gum.

Mom's voice was chirping on about how her husband had died and how she had so much to do to take care of her son (not me, of course). No one seemed the slightest bit interested in Mom's banter, but it was the first time she verbally acknowledged that her husband had died.

Mae came over to Mom and said, "Bertha, it's your turn," whereupon Mom took this opportunity to introduce me. "Mae, this is my other son, Joe." My father's name was Joe, but I ignored her mistake.

I smiled and took my seat, hoping my mother never had the opportunity to introduce me to the president of the United States.

I found it so intriguing that there were five older women in this salon and the moment one left, another one was coming in as if cued for entry, each of the same demographics.

Looking at them, I wondered how they might have looked when they first fell in love … tasted their first kiss, and discovered the depth of passion for the first time. I wondered if they even remembered. My eyes returned to Mom, and the same questions I had applied to the other women whom I never seen before this morning were about Mom. I wondered, *What was Mom like before she met Dad?* The question would be partially answered in the years to come as Mom's dementia would unveil pieces of her past, imagined or not, that would tell me far more about her than I ever expected to know.

Returning to all the women of advanced age in the salon—excuse me, beauty parlor—my heart hoped their respective memories were strong in each of them. I wanted them to recall the emotions of when the spring crispness emerged

15

from winter or what thoughts rushed to their hearts when they saw a full moon in a star-filled sky. I prayed their memories included summer walks and holding hands with a handsome boy whose very presence made them feel like the most beautiful woman in the world. I hoped there were songs that filled their ears that reminded them of a slow dance shared at the town block dance.

What must these women, and my mother, have looked like fifty or sixty years ago? What were their expectations for the lives before them? How did they approach each day?

When they sat in those chairs forty or fifty years earlier, were they getting their hair done for a sister's wedding? Was their tall and dashing beau coming home from his hitch in the service? Maybe it was the high school formal. Whatever the long ago occasion was, surely there was an excitement about that special moment when a hairdresser would complete her magic. Did the hairdresser hand a mirror to the then young woman? Did she see a new color, a new style, a perfect set, and most importantly a new, fresh, and sparkling girl? I couldn't help but imagine how many times each of these ladies had sat in these same chairs, filled with anticipation and excitement.

I wondered about all these things. I looked over at Mom leafing through the *National Enquirer.* I remembered how beautiful she was and how handsome Dad was so many years ago.

I allowed myself to drift nostalgically, recalling just for a second how life was once a ball and a bat, a pile of fallen leaves, the smell of freshly cut green grass, and the musical moments with Mom on the little hardwood floor in our home.

I remembered my brother, curly haired, fun, someone to talk to, someone to kid with, someone to watch Thursday night television shows with as we waited for Mom and Dad to arrive home from their Thursday night shopping. Would Mom sneak the purchase of a candy bar for each of us? As the car pulled into the driveway, we thought maybe Mom had a Three Musketeer bar or a box of Good-N-Plenty.

We never connected these special treats to the Novocain-less cavity drilling we both suffered through when we were lost in the joy of devouring those iconic candy types of the 1950s. It was all so simple and routine. At that moment I returned back in time with these older women again, thinking of their thoughts of better times and their lives yet to be lived, rather than the life already lived.

Their faces, especially my mother's, reflected age. Each line in each face surely was the result of the anguish of worry and the pain of life's losing moments when loved ones were lost and departed from our lives with the speed of a hummingbird's wings.

As I watched with increasing interest, I witnessed fleeting smiles. Within their squinting eyes was the twinkle of life and the hope of a good day to come. Maybe a good day was one free from physical pain, an effortless trip to the bathroom, a tasty meal, a favorite soap opera, or a visit from their grandchildren.

Indeed, their expectations had changed as all things change, but now as I tried to read their thoughts and guess their history, I celebrated their lives.

God bless them all, I say, because this is true, as long as the heart can pump its life-giving blood and a single memory lingers in the brain, there is hope for tomorrow.

I was embarking on a decade of love with my mother when I would need to cling to this edict. Alzheimer's/dementia would take her mind and then her body, but as long as I kept her memories, real or imagined, alive, her life would be worth living.

As I left the beauty parlor with Mom, who beamed with her new hairdo, it was I who had received the real "makeover." As if waking up one day with perfect eyesight, I saw my mother through different eyes. I felt a new dynamic of love. There was a need to be more sensitive and caring. My heart and eyes were working in concert with Mom, and God had a answered my prayer.

Son's Rule: The hours, days, and years with a parent with Alzheimer's/dementia will have many challenges that will tear at your heart, mind, and soul. Try to remember that in the

Stephen W. Hoag, Ph.D.

end, you will come to cherish your own days with embracing hands. You will breathe a little freer. You will smile a little easier. Most importantly, you will find yourself seeking the passion of life more than ever because you can now, where before you couldn't. In this way your father or mother will teach you the most important lesson of life right to the end of his or her life.

Chapter 5

You Were Always
the Homely One

My brother, Tommy, was identified as retarded early in life, but at a time in education history (1950s) when no local programs were available to educate or guide them through the specific challenges of child-to-adult development, let alone the specific mental limitations of individual retarded children. Beyond the academic skills to read and write, the 1950s seemed to be a decade when the schools would just herd those identified as mentally retarded in a single classroom without regard to age or levels of retardation.

My parents were never quite comfortable with Tommy's quiet demeanor, lack of attention, or seeming shortage of male characteristics. For Dad, that meant "making a man" out of him and me to a different degree. This meant a daily dose of regimentation, derogatory name calling, and often severe beatings. There were constant references to "when I was a lad," or "back in the service," which were always a prelude to harshly critical comments such as "you will always be useless," and "you're so dumb you can't get out of your own way."

It is important to identify two key background factors. First, Dad was one of seven brothers who were all rough and tumble Irishmen, under the strict hand of their father, my grandfather. Growing up in Pittston, Pennsylvania, my father and his brothers had a boxing ring in the backyard behind

19

the rose trestles, where disputes were often settled. Described in glib conversations by my uncles during our infrequent trips to Pittston as a young boy to see my grandparents, the brutality scared me.

I'm glad my brother doesn't remember those dinner table depictions of fistfights in the backyard during my father's youth. Dad, the oldest of the sons, was probably raised with a bit more scrutiny, certainly with a "swing first" mentally.

The second childhood factor worth noting was that Dad probably didn't have a childhood. As soon as he could carry a shovel, he was required to work after school in the coal mines that stood only a few hundred yards beyond the railroad tracks above their house on Center Street. Dad barely got through the eighth grade. With the Depression engulfing his generation of children, Dad was summarily enlisted by his father into the Civilian Conservation Corps (CCC) at age fifteen.

Under any circumstances, I don't know how my grandparents sent their eldest son away for what turned out to be years, beginning at the age of fifteen. My mother told me my grandfather lied about my father's age when they enlisted him in the CCC. I remember a conversation Mom and I had about the Depression. She told me everyone, child and adult, did almost anything they could to get money to support their families. Even considering the desperation of those times, the thought of saying good-bye to a child at so early at age is much beyond my understanding. Dad must have been terrified traveling for days on trains and buses to get to Tennessee where he was stationed for almost two years.

I can only imagine how tough he had to be or become to survive the circumstances of those New Deal work camps. So, although I am not making a single excuse for Dad and the manner in which he treated us, one and all, his childhood makes the case for why he was such a mean-spirited man.

Consequently, Mom was the "big compensator." Growing up, she always increased her rate of attention to us when we were the object of one of Dad's tirades. Dad was unpredictable. He could turn from asleep on the couch to instantly awake and threatening. The only time he was predictable was when he was drinking. Then he was downright terrifying and seemingly unaware of how hard he was hitting us. Mom left him twice due to his drinking because it always led to ruthless behavior.

Like an abused dog who will often flinch or cower at a sudden movement or loud noise, Tommy and I would dash to our room, or into the kitchen where Mom usually would be, when we heard Dad pull up to the house. If we were outside and saw him pull into the driveway, we had space, or a buffer zone I guess, so we just stayed out of sight. That didn't stop him from directing venom at us if he had been drinking or had had a tough day at the factory. If Mom sensed something by the way he closed a door or took off his work boots, the three of us would go out the back screen door to the cement steps at the back of the house. There Mom would turn on an instant smile and play one of her "made-up games," as she called them. These were games she extemporaneously created to distract or entertain us, using any object that might be lying around.

Tommy was particularly affected by the potential of being yelled at or hit. He always seemed to be stooped over a little and rarely stood up straight, even though Mom continually insisted, "Stand up tall, Tommy." I guess the three of us were in a daily state of terror, but what I remember most is how it all affected Tommy. His eyes never looked up, his shoulders were stooped, and his voice was so quiet.

Mom would ask to look at my neck, back, and shoulders from time to time. I never quite understood why, but once I got to high school she stopped doing that. I asked her once why she had done that and she got rather angry with me for asking. That seemed screwy to me, so one day I asked my aunt Fanny, who was my mother's closest sister. She told me never to ask my mother again because it was my mother checking for bruises and cuts.

The only lasting physical scar Tommy or I have is the one on my hairline, where Dad pushed my head against the wall and opened up a cut that required stitches. Mom called our doctor, who came to the house and stitched me up. Doctors did that sort of thing in those years, but the reason he came to the house is that Mom wouldn't leave my brother alone with Dad. The real lasting scars lay inside my brother—emotional consequences of being subjected to almost-daily violence. What is forever interesting is how, despite all Tommy went through with Dad, he loved Dad so much.

Mom had a wonderful knack of compensating for what Dad did and oftentimes didn't do. This was especially apparent for Tommy. Mom considered me "smart," which was a nebulous term she used for meaning "not retarded."

Mom looked for every good thing about Tommy and highlighted it. She had an enthusiastic compliment for him for everything he did, small or large. If Tommy stood up straight, she would kiss him on both cheeks. If Tommy drew a picture of some kind (and Tommy was rather artistic), she would show it to the neighbors and tell him over and over how talented he was. Conversely, I could have accompanied Alan Shepard into space, and Mom would have said, "That's nice." I still detest the word "nice" in any context.

However, there was one thing that started early in our lives that followed us almost to the end of her life. Since we were kids, Mom would call Tommy the *handsome one.* "Look how handsome Tommy is in this photo," she would proclaim to visiting neighbors and her sisters. And if someone would enquire, "How about Stevie?" Mom would casually state, "Stevie was always a little homely."

I had been called "homely" by her so many times that I actually began to believe I was, or am. It is interesting how you don't think of the things your parents call you as kids. You just get used to it and sometimes refer to yourself by those nicknames or descriptors. However, the homely thing would rear its ugly head in those last ten years with Mom.

Following dad's death and in the early stages of dementia, Mom went out with me, sometimes daily, as she expected me to assume Dad's duties as chauffeur. I was rather glad to accommodate, although sometimes those requests for transportation came at rather inopportune times.

The manifestations of Alzheimer's/dementia would often take her basic salutary conversations with people we would meet along the way to something less than comfortable moments. Noting an event from my chronicle from 2004, Mom and I attended a yard sale. Mom and Dad loved those "sell your junk to someone" occasions. I was always turned off by even touching someone else's collected scrap. In escorting Mom to these yard sales, I began to realize that this was an opportunity for her to socialize, so I was happy about that.

On this particular occasion she ran into someone who knew her from the senior citizen center, and right away she introduced me as her "other son, Stevie." She explains that Tommy, her older, good-looking son, was home, and introduced me as "this son," the "homely one." This evoked a giggle from the woman as I just smiled coyly with an acknowledging nod. If my usual oral glibness were to have come out, I would have responded, "Nice to meet you. I'm 'Homely Hoag.' Where are the ugly people sitting?"

The second moment occurred at the Shop & Shop supermarket, the location of so many "mom and Stevie" moments in our walk with dementia. We were making our laps around the aisles, and at the top of aisle four near the poultry, an elderly woman yelled out, "Bertha!"

Mom turned around, and I knew she didn't recognize the woman, but she said hello. The woman began with the usual comments relative to how good Mom looked and asked, "How is Joe [my departed father]?"

Mom casually responded in her typical droll manner: "Joe died; how are you?" So much for lamentations.

So the woman with bluish-green hair looked at me and said, "This must be your good-looking son, Tom."

Mother quickly responded, "Noooo, this is Stevie, the homely one."

Smiling, I tried to put on my "oh my, I am homely" look, but I just took a big breath and smiled.

The woman dropped her eyes and tried not to laugh as I turned to my right to see if Stop and Shop had any wild boar left on the shelf, a sustaining food for homely folks.

Looking back to my high school years, it would be easy to blame Mom or Dad for a ton of my missteps and malfunctions, but I never did. I was rather unsuccessful, to say the least, with young ladies in high school, holding my high school's all-time record for most invitations made to different girls to attend the senior prom with me without an affirmative response. There were seven girls I asked to go to the prom with, including the foreign exchange student. Even when I grew very sick with a thyroid condition that did in fact change my appearance and energy level in high school and into college, I never looked at my folks as so many people do these days and blame it on them. So maybe there was something to this "homely" thing Mom hung on me.

In 2009 I had engaged the Companions and Homemakers organization to bring in some people each week to help with the cleaning of the house and cleaning Mom. These women were, for the most part, really easy to work with, although Mom insisted I fire most of them. The best of them all was Chelsea, a forever smiling young lady with a gentle, loving voice and never a negative word.

By 2010 Mom had long since forgotten my name, but Chelsea and I would always ask her, "Who is this"? I never gave up wanting to hear my mom say my name. One evening, with Mom sitting at the kitchen table after Chelsea had given her a bath, I sat across from her making small talk with her. Enlisting any level of discourse with someone with dementia about any subject is necessary as long as it was responsive.

I asked Mom every few minutes, "Who am I?".

Mom would respond with various names of people of her past who I had roll-played over the years (see Chapter 10, "What's My Name?"). This evening I just wanted to hear my name, Steve. It must have sounded to Chelsea that I was becoming frustrated, because Chelsea tried to help.

She knelt next to Mom and said to her, "Who is that, Bertha? C'mon, you know who that is." Mom said some of her more common names of deceased relatives like "Fanny ... Dora ... Sam?"

Chelsea was doing all she could to press the right button to have Mom say my name. Finally, Chelsea raised her voice just a decibel and said, "Bertha, that's your son. Who is it?"

Mom lifted her head and looked at me with those light-blue eyes of hers, and said, "Homely."

SON'S RULE: No matter how little logic and frame of reference you think your parent with dementia still possesses, be careful not to expect simple answers to simple questions. You may have your own remaining ego pinched with a response that was always there, and you may not want to hear it.

Chapter 6

Sing, Stevie, Sing

Music was always a significant component of our mother-son relationship. Actually, before there was a me, there was music ordained for me by my parents.

To provide context to what eventually was a rather happy aspect of our shared challenges with Alzheimer/dementia experiences as mother and son, it is important to understand a little history.

Mother and Dad met at a USO show at Fort Devens, Massachusetts, in 1943. From all Mom told me and seeing the photos of those times, big bands were always performing at Devens.

Many of these traveling swing bands solicited the support of local musicians, dancers, and singers if they were of sufficient talent and skill to be quickly acclimated to the band's repertoire. Mom was a talented dancer and singer, as was her sister Dorothy. Mom jumped at any opportunity to perform at these USO shows, and there she met my father, who served in a number of military units prior to and during World War II. Besides being a rather feisty and short-tempered member of the 101st Airborne and the Army Corps of Engineers, he could play the trumpet rather well.

As my mother always had a thing for red-haired men, her attraction to him was predictable. Mom and Dad's generation seems to be rather protective when it comes to any discussion of intimacy, wartime/combat experiences, and finances. However, Mom had saved through all these years all of Dad's letters he had written from England, France, and a few other countries where he'd served.

While Dad was not an educated man, with rather sketchy information as to whether he ever completed the eighth grade, his penmanship was magnificent. In these letters Dad talked about wanting to marry Mom when he returned and how they would make their sons and daughters (he didn't get any girls) musicians and performers. His words described how Mom would teach their children to dance and sing. That was precisely what she did with me.

My earliest recollections of life are all backdropped by a blanket of music. Our rented housing project home was tiny by any standards with limited space, but the hardwood floor was always shiny and devoid of any furniture. The big radio set containing a wire recorder in the corner of our parlor was the largest piece of furniture we owned and seemed to shrink the room. The secondhand couch and one chair were at the perimeter of the room, as Mom and Dad always kept the hardwood floor free of any obstacle.

Dad would come home from his work at the factory extremely dirty and savagely odorous, and his conduct was often harsh and violent, but he would not walk on that tiny wood floor with his work boots. There was something sacred about that patch of floor as I came to understand during my early life. It was on that floor that Mom would take me by my hands and show me the rudiments of tap dancing and selling a song with your hands and body movements.

She would always tell me, "To dance, you must use each part of your foot ... the toe for this, the heel for that." That little patch of floor was a stage in her eyes, a classroom for performing. I didn't even realize that I was doing it. I just did it because it pleased her. She always smiled when we were on the floor. It was our little stage. I never realized until many years later how little else made her smile.

No day of my early life was absent music. That Philco radio was always turned on. I remember so often walking home from elementary school, and as I crossed Backes Court, our neighborhood, where we lived on the corner, I could hear the music coming from the window our house. If there was a song that Mom particularly liked, she would teach it to me almost from the moment I returned home. I fondly recall her running out of the house one day to meet me at the corner. She was all giddy and demanded I run to the house because a certain song was on the radio and she wanted me to hear it. Other than weekends, when Dad's presence meant the three of us (Mom, Tom, and me), were seen and not heard, there was rarely a day when Mom didn't sing and dance with me. Tommy often would watch, but rhythm wasn't natural to him like many other things.

If I wanted to get out of the house after I got home from school to go play with my friends, I'd better be ready to sing first. I learned quickly that just going through the motions of singing a song to placate my mother didn't work. Not that she was ever tough with me, but she was so enthusiastic about my singing that I just had to please her. So the key was to sing it right on the first attempt, and that meant I had to stand in the middle of the room, move my body, arms, and hands as she taught me, and be loud. She insisted I smile whenever I sang or danced.

I would ask her why I should smile when some songs were more serious or "bee-bop" in nature. Her position was always that I wasn't a very handsome boy, and I must compensate so the audience won't notice. Actually, as you've read, she used the adjective "homely" to describe my facial status. So I smiled whenever I sang.

To be sure, the greatest joy I ever gave my mother was performing.

She taught me so many different varieties of music, from Jewish songs such as "Romania" to the early songs of rock and roll, like "Sh-Boom" or "Singing the Blues," to the more avant-garde club songs of Belle Barth.

Mom would always ask (more like insist) that I, at four or five years old, sing for any person who came to the house. If there was company, I sang. When we walked together to the bank, the post office, the town hall, or just out to walk along a tree-lined road, I sang. What made it fun was Mom's smile. Mom once allowed a door-to-door Fuller Brush salesman to enter the house and had me sing a song for him. When I finished singing, she immediately asked him to leave before he got his suitcase of wares open.

Looking back, the time we shared in some manifestation of musical performance was her escape from the harsh circumstances she endured.

There was so much anger and violence in those first twelve years of my life as Dad drank, and when he drank he looked for someone to hit. It was Mom or Tommy and me or all three. As the sun set each day, tensions rose as Dad looked for the smallest excuse to begin the beatings. We all took it, and unfortunately, Tommy took the brunt of it each night. When Mom—never more than one hundred pounds—tried to block the door to our bedroom or stand between me and my dad, she was summarily removed.

We lived in the 1950s, when domestic issues were never discussed in public and even neighbors who lived within fifty feet of us and heard the yelling would never interfere (despite the fact that two of our two closest neighbors on either side were policemen). There was no protection, so we learned to never cry, scream, or complain. My friends would see the bruises, as did my elementary school teachers, but no one ever asked about their origin.

When I was seven I made my first public appearance singing a song entirely in Yiddish to the Sisters of Hadassah. As Mom often did in my youth, she borrowed a jacket, shirt, and tie from the neighbors so I looked as good as a little boy could look. Wearing other children's clothes was something that always happened when Mom took me somewhere to sing.

When she took me by bus to a concert at Woolsey Hall at Yale University or to meet a singing teacher in New Haven, she would insist I sing to the passengers. If we were waiting for a bus to take us back to town and a crowd of any size was about, she had me sing. I don't recall ever protesting or balking at the request, I just got used to doing it.

It got so that every time a group of people were around me, even when Mom wasn't there, I felt I should sing. This meant involving my voice, body, hands, and feet.

This actually got me into trouble in the fall of 1959 as a fourth-grade student at Simpson School. Each morning, all students were required to sit quietly on the front steps of the school and wait for our teacher to open the door. Only in the case of rain were we allowed to just walk in.

For explanation sake, my fourth-grade teacher, who will go nameless, believed in high levels of corporal punishment from everything from smudging your math paper to throwing up in class.

So here I was sitting on the bottom step of the long staircase leading to the front door. All the kids sat there being as quiet as possible. It was a typical spring day, full of sun, a little nip in the air, and here I was sitting in the front row of an ascending cement staircase full of kids—an audience. So I stood up, turned toward my fellow students, and whipped into a full emotional rendition of "It's Only Make Believe," by Conway Twitty. I sang it the way Mom taught me, and lo and behold, kids my age were actually listening. I was no longer singing to older women or random crowds. I was singing to children my own age and felt great doing it.

I never saw the door at the top of the stairs open; no one did. However, there was a high-pitched scream, followed by, "What are you doing? *Shut up!*"

I immediately stopped, whereupon my teacher beckoned me to the top of the stairs.

She immediately grabbed my ear and pulled me down the hallway. I was terrified. The entire way she yelled at me, and kept saying, "How dare you? How dare you?"

When we got the classroom, she pushed me through door. As I got up she pushed me into a desk and then grabbed my ear again, leading me to the coat closet at the back of the room. There she continued to call me names, most of which I didn't understand, and pushed me into the small closet, the empty hangers hitting my head.

She told me my punishment was to stand in the closet all day with the door closed without making a sound. I was nine years old. I didn't understand what I had done that was wrong, but from my upbringing with Dad, I knew not to cry.

There I remained in the closet all day. I heard all the kids come into class. The teacher taught class as usual. Then they all went to lunch as usual, followed later by afternoon recess as usual. Then they were dismissed at three thirty. I heard them leave. I had been standing the entire time. I had to go the bathroom—badly. The teacher did not come to let me out. Finally my need to go to the bathroom had reached a breaking point.

I slowly opened the door to a darkened classroom. I rushed out the door and ran directly to the boys' room. A janitor was cleaning in there and I used the first commode I saw. He asked me what I was doing in the school this late and said it was after four.

Relieved, I ran down the hallway and out the door. It was then as I walked down the stairs that I started to cry. I didn't cry much as a kid, but I remember crying then. I walked down Center Street to Simpson Avenue. About halfway home I saw my mom walking toward me. I ran to her and hugged her and cried.

She told me my teacher called her and told me what happened. I immediately said I was sorry, and she told me not to cry. I asked her if she was going to tell Dad, and she assured me she would never tell him. That was a greater relief than getting to the lavatory before I wet myself. There was a big weeping willow on Simpson Avenue, and she told me to sit down beside it with her for a moment. *I knew it,* I thought. *Here it comes. Mom is going to yell at me,* but she never yelled. I didn't think I could take a rebuke from her.

We sat there quietly for a few minutes and I started speak, but she shushed me. Now, I knew I was about to get balled out.

Mom turned to me and said, "I want to know only one thing." She spoke directly. "Were you good?"

I said, "No, Mom, I wasn't good. I got into trouble."

31

Then she got loud with me: *"How did you sing?"*

I was so shell-shocked and my mother had just asked me how I sang?

"Okay, I guess," I said or something to that effect.

That opened the floodgates. From there she peppered me with a battery of questions, including, "Did you use your hands in front of you?" "Did you look into their eyes?" "Did everyone in the audience hear you?"

I don't remember how I answered, but Mom told me she wanted me to perform that song for her when we are alone, so she could see how I did it.

We didn't talk for a bit as we restarted our walk home from the willow tree. We were almost home when our next-door neighbor approached us and enquired about what had happened. Her daughter, who was a fifth grader at the school, had obviously told her.

Mom told the neighbor not to tell Joe (Dad). That was a key strategy to avoid a beating of biblical proportions for a problem in school. The neighbor, a woman who meant well and seemed to talk constantly, asked me casually about the *closet*. My mother stopped, turned to me, and said, "What about the closet?"

The neighbor never let me get the words out. She proceeds to tell Mom that I'd had to stand in a closed closet from nine until three thirty. Apparently, my teacher never mentioned to my mother the manner in which I was punished. I was nine years old and wanted this nightmare to be over, but the blabbermouth neighbor extended the event with her description of my punishment.

We arrived home, and Mom never asked me about the incarceration in the closet. Later that evening, the neighbor's daughter who was the fifth-grade student came to the back screen door. Mom saw her and rushed to cut her off as Dad was sitting at the kitchen table in a typical nasty mood. I joined Mom going out the door as she explained to the little girl not to talk about this around Mr. Hoag. I was looking to find a neighbor to play catch with after the narrow escape from a potential "Daddy beating," and I heard Mom ask the girl, "Did you hear Stevie sing?"

You had to hand it to my mother. She had her priorities straight. Don't worry about a little closet time for Stevie as long he entertained the student body.

Although I continued to perform in various venues throughout high school, college, and beyond, I chose to follow a different professional path. I disappointed mother very much, and it was only when she became afflicted with Alzheimer's disease that I discovered the real depth of her disappointment.

My mother really never acknowledged what I did for a living. Even in some of the most victorious moments of my life when honors and awards would come my way, she would downplay them or just ignore them completely. Yes, it hurt at times, but I understood that she held out hope that I would one day come to my senses and get involved in the performing arts.

As the decades passed, every so often mother would lay one of her rapier-like pieces of sarcasm, designed to evoke guilt in my gut about my chosen profession in education.

I would bob and weave or change the subject, but I knew she would have loved to see me do something with everything she'd taught me. Actually, with all the public speaking I have done throughout my life, few who know me could argue that her efforts were wasted.

Then in an "all-of-sudden" moment (June 23, 2002, when Dad died), Mom was mine to care for, with Alzheimer's/ dementia tugging at her elbow. Among the many aspects of our shared history that would seep into the fabric of what we addressed with this often perception-bending, memory-altering Alzheimer's disease, my musical upbringing was never far from the daily *"Playbill."*

After Dad died, the weekly trips to Stop & Shop on Thursday evenings were permanently placed on my schedule. This meant I would accompany her, picking her up at precisely five thirty p.m.

Although there are considerable anecdotes about our shopping, the musical interludes are the most profound. Part of the early symptoms of dementia include the loss of social skills and personality changes. Mom's personality went from soft-spoken with never-a-curse-word uttered to a no-hold's-barred, brassy, sometimes crude little woman. Forever one to drop the guilt statements with a highly polished degree of sarcasm, she now was armed with the bombast of General Patton.

The experience of shopping with Mom included dramatic moments of great candor, when she would spontaneously speak out—loudly—on the physical features of the Stop & Shop patrons, or express any thought or emotion that darted across her mind.

With me as her escort on these weekly food-shopping excursions, I could momentarily be her husband, Joe; her long-since departed brother, Sam; or her son, Stevie. But not Stevie, her current son in his fifties. Not him. I was Stevie, the little homely kid who sang and danced at Mom's behest.

It was all kind of interesting at first. I just smiled as I walked behind her, with her manning the shopping cart for balance. She would say hello to almost anyone she saw. She thought she knew everyone. If she remembered that I was there, she would say something akin to, "Hello, this is my little son, Stevie." If she let it stop there I was happy as a clam.

As time went on and the symptoms of dementia became more provocative, she would say just about anything about me. Among these serious one-line introductions were "This is Stevie. He isn't much to look at it, but he has twin daughters," "This is Stevie. He's good scout. He likes girls," or "This is Stevie. You should see my other son. He's handsome."

What really endures were the not-so-few Thursday shopping nights when she would insist I sing for her on the spot.

You must understand, she would never accept a little-voiced whispered rendition of the song she requested. She expected a performance to the standard she had taught me those many years ago.

On May 19, 2005, as the symptoms of Alzheimer's with respect to delusions had increased, we entered the aisle where the frozen foods were located (the aisle I called "Murder's Row" because mom would take more than thirty minutes there). She liked to open every refrigerated case door and read the contents of almost every frozen food box.

On this evening, a woman and her daughter were trying to gain access to the same glass door as the one Mom was standing in front of as she pulled down one box after another. I gently tapped her on the shoulder, asking her to move over so these folks could select something from the case.

She turned around, flashed a smile at the mother and daughter, and said loudly, "Is it curtain time already?" I had no idea where this was going.   With that, she remained standing in front of the open case and slightly pushed me, saying, "You're on!"

I instantly got right in her face and whispered to stop and move on. Bad move! Now Mom got all indignant, saying, "Stevie, *you sing for these people now!*"

The scene got worse. Other people were in the aisle and all came over to see what all the yelling was about. I was instantly concerned that this could get out of hand if I got in any way pushy with Mom. She didn't respond to anyone giving her orders since the onset of Alzheimer's. You could ask her health-care workers. Mom could get ornery.

I tried once again to whisper to her with a smile. Again, she blurted, "Stevie, you get out there and sing. I'll be here."

So now the new onlookers who'd heard the commotion were watching. One elderly man yelled out, "Sing—go ahead, sing."

I was screwed and I knew it. With that, I stepped back ... and asked Mom with a smile, "What would you like me to sing?"

"Sing the mermaid song," she proclaimed. "Everyone likes when you do that one."

Not thinking about the mild sexual overtones of the requested song, I occupied my little space in the aisle. With that, my hands began to rise from my sides as Mom taught me and I began an a cappella rendition of "Minnie the Mermaid."

The instant I began to sing, I saw my then ninety-one-year-old mother smile broadly. I hadn't seen that smile in a long time. Mom held on to the shopping cart with one hand, the frozen food door with the other, moving her hips to my song as she did when I was a child.

The smile she flashed made all the challenges with her Alzheimer's and care seem so insignificant.

I sang. I finished the song. I got a little generous applause. I got my mother redirected and moved her and the basket of groceries to the checkout counter post haste.

Over the next four years I would sing again at Stop & Shop, more than a few times. Every now and then when I shop there, someone will approach me and remind me of the time he or she heard me sing for my mother. I don't remember the people who surrounded us during those rather spontaneous musical moments. I only remember Mom, which is as it should be.

As the disease's impact on her increased, Mom never stopped asking me to sing for her. I sang in doctors' offices, hospitals, in her bedroom, at meal times, and even while bathing her. In retrospect, my mother trained me that I would perform for her when she needed me most. As much as I'd disappointed her in not pursing any type of involvement with music, it is clear now that my best performances were at her side.

The last time I sang for her was on a Thursday, January 5, 2012, after shopping for her and Tommy. She died the next day, January 6, 2012.

The song I sang to her that last night was "Minnie the Mermaid."

Son's Rule: God gives you a set of blessings and some Divine tools. They are designed for you to love your parent with Alzheimer's in the most perfect way possible. You may never fully understand what those gifts are while your parent is alive, but they are exactly what your mom or dad needs most, and ready to be used precisely when he or she needs it.

Chapter 7

The Case of the Stolen Wine Glasses

Less than a year after Dad died, Mom's deportment, especially with me, began to change rather dramatically. With Dad's passing I felt Mom and Tommy would need more support than ever before. Mom and Dad were married for fifty-two years, although during the last few years of Dad's life they seemed less connected with each other. Since Dad's retirement in 1978, they were always getting in the car and going somewhere. Not a day went by that they weren't going to the senior citizen center, driving to a local rummage sale, or going food shopping. Stop & Shop must have loved them because they would visit that store two or three times a week, sometimes buying nothing. However, the last two years of Dad's life, Mom and Dad didn't talk much.

So when Dad died, I increased my time with Mom, believing she would miss Dad a lot and need me more. As I do tend to overdo things in life, I was spending a great deal of time with her each day. Within a few weeks of my increased "Mommy time," she started to blame me for all sorts of crazy things.

At this time I had taken her to a psychologist who dealt with older women and specialized in grief management. The doctor didn't sense that Mom was grief-stricken about Dad. Rather, he felt Mom was having a difficult time remembering who her husband was. In the discussions with the doctor, she wanted to talk about her sisters, some who had died more than fifty years ago. The doctor concluded the obvious: that mom had Alzheimer's/dementia and it was moving along rapidly.

When I asked him about the best course of action, he stated what would become a familiar refrain for almost everyone around me: "Consider putting your mother in a nursing home."

There was enough left of Mom's rational thinking skills to ask her what she wanted to do. At that time along the dementia highway, Mom would say she wasn't leaving Tommy. As time went on, she would curtly say, "No one is taking me from my house."

It was easier at that time to try to remain objective in my approach to Mom and the complicated circumstances that surrounded her. I had always drawn some degree of satisfaction in my ability to compartmentalize my life. I worked hard not to let one aspect affect another, opening and closing doors to daily tasks and relationships. It was my way of trying to stay balanced in my private and professional worlds of high energy and emotion. Following Dad's death and the subsequent responsibilities for Mom and Tommy, I was to find out that my sense of balance had lost its gyroscope. Better said: welcome to the world of dementia.

During this early stage, Mom had spontaneous shout-outs of blaming me for most of the ills of the world, but the accusations that initially seemed almost laughable were super serious to her as I was quick to discover.

There were her accusations of taking some item from the house without her permission, oftentimes barking at me for something I'd better not do.

If she was in bed and heard me come in the house, she would yell out, *"Stay out of the cellar—I don't want you touching my things!"*

I was blamed for hiding her breakfast spoon; throwing out last night's *Sentinel* (the newspaper of her childhood newspaper in Fitchburg, Massachusetts), and entering the "little room," the room in the house where all junk and photographs of the past went to hide.

In the winter of 2004 the "blame game" reached its zenith. I received a call from Mom at eleven a.m. while I was at the office in Hartford. Without saying hello, she bellowed out that she'd called the police because I had stolen her wine glasses.

"You did what?" I yelled. Suffice to say, I was out and into my car in moments. As I tore down I-91, I was angered, embarrassed, and confused. It then occurred to me that Mom and Dad never had any wine glasses, at least none I ever saw. It didn't kick in right away in my pragmatic brain that this "wine glass theft" was a product of the dementia. I was just worried about being humiliated.

I arrived forty-five minutes later, and a police car was outside the house. Wondering where this was going to lead, I entered the house, and the police officer was sitting across from Mom at the kitchen table as she slurped her morning cereal and milk. She was having a rather lighthearted conversation with the officer about the cat, who was sitting on the table.

After a few uncomfortable moments, the police officer got Mom to respond to a question describing the wine glasses that were purportedly stolen.

Mom looked at the officer with this squinty glare and said, "That's just a silly question. Where did you learn how to be a cop?" Then she threw her left hand up and said, "Ask my son. He took them. He can tell you what they look like."

The officer asked her a few other questions relative to where the glasses were kept and what color they were. Once again Mom deferred to me to give all the details of the glasses. The officer was getting the picture that Mom was "out there in never-never dementia land."

He thanked Mom for her time and asked me to walk him out. He was smiling as we exited, and I said nothing. He asked me how long she had been like this. I glibly said, "A couple of hours."

He then looked at me, wished me good luck, and left shaking his head.

Upon entering the house again, I considered issuing a stern rebuke to Mom for doing such a stupid, embarrassing thing, but when I saw the cat with one leg in Mom's cereal bowl as Mom continued to eat her breakfast, I could only kiss her on her head and sit down.

Son's Rule: As you learn the tenuous rules of dementia, consider that real people will sometimes become involved with imagined events. Remember, when accusations come your way, there is no due process of law in the thoughts of a parent with dementia.

Chapter 8

Bath Time for Bertha

The early years with Mom (2002–05), as she began to experience the increasing impact of Alzheimer's/dementia, were challenging in their own way, but nothing brought about my booming oral proclamation that "This was *not* in the son's handbook" more than when I began to assist her with a unique brand of toilet training and the act of bathing.

I never quite gave up hope that I could stop the rages of Alzheimer's/dementia. With the downward spiral of the disease, a little bit of her human dignity was being chipped away with each passing week and month. I cannot speak for others with this affliction, but Mom fought to hold on to those daily tasks and normal activities that make up a person's identity and some semblance of personal independence.

Of all the clichés regarding advanced age, the one that does not apply to those with Alzheimer's/dementia is "aging gracefully." There is little grace for someone who has lived a life serving her family while maintaining a standard of poise and modesty to now being stripped of the ability to care for her own bodily needs. The simple tasks such as brushing her own hair or teeth to the more complicated undertakings of bathing became more problematic and visibly frustrating for Mom as time moved along.

One of the blessings of those years was that I watched her intently when I was with her. I really paid attention to the little things. I know I never looked that closely before. It also pained me to watch her struggle.

This was a woman who found a way to remain married with a difficult spouse for more than fifty years. This was a woman who raised a handicapped child to adulthood after a school system failed him and with a husband who could never fully understand and accept Tommy's retardation. She never raised her voice or blamed the school, Dad, or God. For sixty years she cared for Tommy in every way. This was a great human being, my mom.

Recognizing what she had endured in her life, I wanted to give her the things that mattered most to her. She wanted to keep Tommy with her for the rest of her life and wanted to live in her own home and die there. By the grace of God, we did that for her. However, there was one more thing she valued, and that turned out to be the hardest thing to give her.

Mom loved to meander down memory lane and wax poetic about her youth. She enjoyed talking about her childhood, her former friends, her sisters, and an endless variety of moments she'd experienced. She wanted to share all her cherished memories with everyone and recall all she was in her youth— pretty, talented, popular, forever Bertha Ethel Bever.

Dementia was nibbling away at those memories, and she fought to keep them. While she battled on that front, she dealt with what was happening to her body. The war with memory she shared with me, asking me to remind her of names, dates, places, etc. The war with her body she insisted on fighting alone. She didn't want to acknowledge or accept the changes to her body.

The most difficult for Mother and me was her incontinence, which began after her heart attack and stroke in 1999. Nurses at the rehabilitation center taught her how to wear adult diapers, which disgusted her, but she complied. Dad was still alive at the time and did his best to care for her after the heart attack, but she would not allow him to assist in her "personal" tasks. Dad purchased the adult diapers or asked me to "pick up a pack of Pampers," but that was it. Mom insisted on her own privacy even in her weakened state after the heart attack.

I knew she was wearing adult diapers, but unless you were looking for a little puffiness around her midsection, you really couldn't tell she was wearing them. She worked to hide them. Like anything of a personal/private nature with your parents, *you really don't want to know* anyway.

From 2000–03, Mom never acknowledged that she even wore diapers. She took care of her personal activities, including bathing, and believe me, I wasn't looking to assist with any manner of discharge or "voiding" (as the boys and girls in the medical profession say). Privacy is part of human integrity, and no person ever wants to lose the capacity to complete the most personal of functions in our human existence.

My mother was as closed-door private as one could get. My father used to leave the bedroom when Mom was getting dressed as she insisted on her privacy. When she was using the bathroom, the only one in the house, she would barricade the door with the dirty clothes hamper just in case someone forgot she was in there.

When Mom became my responsibility, she was still able to take care of her personal duties, or at least I thought so. I wanted to believe she always would. After all, she wouldn't allow me to participate in any of her personal care anyway.

Then in another of these "all-of-sudden" moments, I arrived after work one day in 2003, trotting upstairs to see Mom in her bed. As I entered the room there was a soiled adult diaper on the floor next to her bed. I wondered how it got there. Who put it there? And what I was supposed to do with it? I just stared at it for a few moments.

Mom was asleep and I didn't want to wake her, so I went back downstairs where Tommy was in the living room, watching television. I asked him, "Tom, did you see the diaper on the floor next to Mommy's bed?"

Tommy, never one to give you anything but a totally honest answer, responded without looking at me, "Stevie? Mommy *stinks.*"

I took that as a big yes. I extended this chat with, "Don't you think you should have picked it up and thrown it out?"

Tommy's forthright answer was, "Mommy *stinks.* You better take her to the emergency room."

I love my brother, but the idea that one lonesome (already used) adult diaper was grounds for a 911 call let me know that I was standing in the middle of *Dementia Island* alone. By the way, did I mention how amazed I was at how heavy these adult diapers were after having been utilized to their fullest?

Without an option, I returned to Mom's room, picked up the hefty diaper, and threw it out, returning with an antiseptic spray bottle and a roll of paper towels as the used diaper left considerable collateral damage on the floor.

Mom scolded me for making too much noise, subsequently waking her up. I quietly told her a diaper was on the floor next to the bed and I was just cleaning it up. I casually and stupidly suggested she should get out of bed and clean herself up. I suppose I embarrassed her, and this represented a *Mom faux pas* from childhood to never mention things that are personal and private.

Then I did something even dumber. To this day, I still can't believe I did it and don't know what I had hoped to accomplish. With my right hand I raised the sheet and blanket, looking to see if she had "made a mess" in the bed and/or on herself.

With that she yelled, *"Get out!"* so loud that Tommy came upstairs and asked me what I was doing to his mother. I quickly defused the situation, assuring Tommy that everything was perfectly all right.

You must remember this was the first time I'd been confronted by a *"Mommy-movement-moment."*

Little did I know I was embarking on one of the most necessary yet repellent activities on our walk with Alzheimer's/dementia.

In 2003 Mom would still not allow anyone to help her with her personal hygiene. Her bed was often wet and needed a regular change of linen and blankets, but she insisted on doing it all herself. I appreciated her insistence to be independent and do things on her own, but I knew it was a matter of time before she would not be able to make a bed, let alone clean herself.

It was time to secure the services of homecare workers to change the bed clothes and do as much as we could get away with in terms of not upsetting her. Things were moving fast, but I was aware of how sensitive she was about her independence. Mom was never cooperative during this period, and with the dementia moving forever forward, this aspect of daily living got progressively worse.

With each day Mom would defecate in her diaper. As I became more involved in this, I realized adult diapers, regardless of the manufacturer, did not include an automatic self-wiping-your-behind mechanism. Someone had to do the cleansing portion of this bodily function. The fact that the person wearing the diaper was usually in a prone position, the distribution of "waste product" was not confined to her behind.

Exacerbating this daily task in the genre of incontinence was that she lost the capacity to sense when she was about to pee or poop, or that she had just completed said movement.

I would often suggest she get up slowly and carefully and go to the bathroom when she felt something strong coming on. In this way, she might avoid the mess that ended up on her body and on the bed. Unfortunately, she never felt a bowel movement coming or knew when she was urinating.

I was not ready to be the one to change my mother's diapers or assist in the endeavor in any way ... not that Mom would ever cooperate anyway. I knew we needed to bring in health-care professionals to bathe and change her during regular intervals of the day. I thought it would be a relatively easy thing to do. You hire someone to come to the house at eight a.m., three p.m., and six p.m. to bathe and change her, and then have the person change and make the bed. Sounds simple, huh?

Alas, it was a daily nightmare. The real obstacle was Mom. She fought me and every health-care worker who came into her bedroom. She screamed, *"Don't touch me!"* and "I can do this myself." Only one health-care worker had the magic we needed. Her name was Chelsea, but she came into our lives a lot later in the decade.

After vetting a number of companies that provided daily health-care workers, I found an agency that showed me great patience, and they needed every ounce of forbearance. Mom was a bear with each of them. She fought almost every care worker I brought in the house, asserting herself with the workers, expressing her displeasure with each of them almost daily, ordering me to "Fire her," or "Get rid of that one."

You must understand that few if any of the care workers wanted to return for a second day after just one with Mom. I came to appreciate how challenging their assignment was once I had to perform certain tasks myself. It was tough to keep a cadre of care workers scheduled each week as many refused to return after a few or even one visit.

Through it all we were able to patch together care workers for the weekdays, but oftentimes on Saturday and Sunday I was usually the only game in town.

My Moment

It was a pretty March day, a Saturday afternoon, and I was out and about running errands. Tommy called me on my seldom-used cell phone to tell me "Mommy is a mess" and I'd better get there and take care of her. Redirecting my plan, I got there as quickly as possible. Upon entering the house, I inhaled the "mess" before I saw it. Mother was sleeping in her bed, and I saw the scope of the problem. It is important to note that up to this point I had never bathed Mom or assisted in this endeavor before.

Did you ever have one of the problems in life that no matter how you approach the problem, there seems to be ten consequences that make the problem even worse? Well, this was one of them.

The first task ... wake Mom. As I didn't want to get any of her "schmutz" on my clothes, I put two towels on the edge of the bed to protect me. That was like using a teaspoon to shovel snow.

I gently shook her. I whispered, "Mom, you have to wake up now."

In anticipated fashion, she replied, "Get away, I'm sleeping."

I was still calm and under control as the fumes of Mother's bedtime defecation were becoming breath *stealing.*

46

Using two hands to shake her awake, she then made these faces like my shaking was causing her great pain. I hadn't seen these facial contortions before. The patience-meter automatically clicked on inside me.

I began to explain the circumstances, which went like this: "Mom, you need to wake up and get to the bathroom. You have pooped in your diapers, and it's all over the place."

Mother grabbed the edge of her blanket, pulled it over her head, and turned away in righteous indignation. As she did, the edge of the blanket pulled up, revealing her sock-covered foot and feces-covered ankle. I realize this was no normal movement. This was a "*four-alarmer.*"

I slowly inched back the blanket from the bottom of the bed toward the head of the bed, and I wanted to yell for help, but I was alone.

I went to the corner of the room and grabbed a large, black plastic bag that I used to carry her dirty laundry to the laundry room in the cellar.

Now armed with the plastic bag and my desire to do whatever was necessary to expeditiously take care of this multifaceted problem, I yanked off the blanket from atop my mother and stuffed it in the bag. Mom immediately yelled that she was cold and to put the blanket that was almost covered in poop back on her.

Unlike the homecare workers, I was not wearing latex gloves or protective outer wear, just a black warm-up suit.

As mom curled in the most snail-like fetal position possible, chanting, "I'm cold, I'm cold, I'm cold," she still hadn't opened her eyes.

My objective was to get her to the bathroom at all costs and to get her into the shower. The details of this grand plan had not yet come to me, but I was prepared to pay any price to get Mom clean. It was such a multifaceted moment. What was about to play out were physical, emotional, and mental tests all coming together at once.

She was covered in her own poop, and the light-blue lace-top nightgown I had bought her for birthday was soaking wet from urine.

With caution to the wind, I wrapped my arms around her and pulled her across to the side of the bed near the door. My warm-up jacket was already covered with my mother's excrement and I no longer cared.

Mom was repeating the same phrases in my ear over and over: "Leave me alone; don't you touch me; put me down." I didn't respond to a single phrase.

With arms wrapped under her armpits as tight as I could around this frail little woman of ninety pounds, I got her to the edge of the bed and asked her to stand up. Her legs were like jelly and I was trying to hold her erect so I could guide her legs with my legs, walking the ten small paces to the bathroom. Try as I might she would let her legs slide down to a sitting position on the floor. I kept lifting her up, but she was ranting and refusing to stand up. This was a new level of indignation. She would not stand up for me, and I was out of options.

As I am not a man of much physical strength, I didn't know if I could do this without her cooperation, but with one swoop, I picked her up in my arms and carried across the threshold of the bathroom. All the while she was killing me with her yelling, "Leave me alone. You're hurting me!"

To make matters even more difficult, Tommy was watching this whole episode. I asked him to help me only once and he made a face and said, "I'm not touching Mom ... she smells." Then Tommy asked casually, "Stevie, do you want me to call 911?" As ridiculous as it may sound, I considered it for a moment. I was really in over my head.

Mom was yelling up a storm with her eyes still shut as we entered the bathroom. I was starting to get the impression that she was doing this on purpose, and I barked, "Mom open your eyes. *Wake up!*" To no avail. She maintained her jelly legs and half-asleep mode.

Having arrived in the bathroom—now what? She was covered with feces from neck to ankle.

Holding her in my arms in the middle of the bathroom and her refusal to stand, I carefully sat her on the commode with the lid thankfully up. She slid back against the lid of the toilet, and I began to pull the urine-soaked nightgown off.

48

Mom was not giving an inch, so with one arm around her I tugged the night gown *off.*

In an all-of-a-sudden moment, Mom realizes she was *naked.* Now the real show began!

All the privacy she insisted upon over the years, all the implied rules exploded with the speed of light. In a split second Mom's eyes were open to their widest, and she was six inches from my face, eyeball to eyeball. The repetitive phases were gone, and she was now screaming, *"Aaaaaaaaaaaaahhhhh!"*

That scared me to the bone. Tommy heard Mother yelling and ran back upstairs, pushed open the door, and started saying, "Mommy's naked, Mommy's naked."

Telling him to go downstairs and relax, I had to do something fast. This situation was getting worse, and now I had an excited, emotional older brother on my hands.

Somehow I had to clean my naked mother. I never wanted to see her naked, but then again I never wanted to have to clean her every body part.

If ever there was a time when I was pleading for God's help *out loud,* this was it. In soliciting the intervention of God, Scripture was flowing out of me.

To reset the scene: my arms were wrapped around Mom, holding her up on the commode, and she was shivering. She was awake and I was right in her face using carefully chosen, unemotionally delivered words: *"Mom ... please ... sit up ... don't move ... give me a minute!"*

She shivered and stared at me but didn't talk. I was thinking this was good. This would give me a few minutes to turn on the water in the bathtub and get it to a temperature that wouldn't burn her sensitive skin and be so cold she had a heart attack.

Mom saw what I was doing. She asked me to get her a clean nightgown. I make the mistake of being honest. "Mom, I have to get you in the bathtub."

"No you don't!" she screamed with a series of threats and insults.

I was running out of time. I had all but forgotten that I was covered in *mom-dirt.* The old bathtub had a hand rail that I'd attached some months ago for her safety, but it now it was a barrier to the task at hand. I pulled it off and tossed it out the door into the hallway.

It was a now-or-never moment as Mom was shivering in her nakedness. I asked her calmly, "Mom, do have to go the bathroom before I give you a bath?"   Bad move!

Mom was firing on all cylinders. "Who do you think you are? Get out! You will *not* give me a bath."

Here I was with bathtub water running, and I reached over to check the temperature with my hand, at the same time trying to explain to my naked mother that she was covered in *schmutz* and I had to clean her up. The water was like the three little bears' porridge: "too hot, too cold, and then just right." The moment was at hand.

With her protestations at their peak, I moved to the side of the toilet, placed my arms under her legs and around her lower back, and lifted her up.

Holding her in my arms, it was clear there was no way to shower or bathe her unless I was actually in the tub with her. What an undesirable reality. I did not have the training of a nurse or homecare worker. It was just me, a son, and there was no Son's Handbook to guide me.

With all manner of prior humility and my previous personal revulsion at the mere thought of seeing my mother naked, I got my arms around her once again. With strength I didn't think I had, I hoisted her up off the commode. She was straining against my efforts and blasting me with an array of insults the like of which I had never heard her say.

My soiled black sneakers came off easily enough before stepping into the tub. Thank God Mom didn't weigh one pound heavier. With her in my arms and me fully clothed, into the tub we went. With greater verbal insistence I demanded she stand. Actually, I shouted. I lowered her to a standing position, but she still required my arm around her waist to hold her up. Without pulling the shower curtain across, I turned the shower spigot on and we both stood in an almost-hot shower together.

50

I can't speak for anyone else. I have no knowledge of any son taking a shower with his ninety-year-old mother. There was no time to consider such things as nudity, modesty, or absurdity. I just wanted to clean my mother as quickly and as safely as possible. The weight of my soaked clothing limited my maneuvering capacity. Mom was facing the shower head with me right behind her, my arm about her waist, and she dug her nails into my arm, screaming, "Take your hands off me!" The moment her feet hit the water, she screamed, "Too cold, too cold! You're trying to kill me!"

I wasted no time. I grabbed the bar of soap and scrubbed every inch of her. Excrement was on her legs and caked all over her back, and I scarcely considered how I would cleanse her most private parts, but it was surely a destination.

With help from the warm water, Mom was becoming clean as I soaped her from the neck down. However, I had to clean parts of her anatomy that I could have never imagined in any scenario. I washed her chest and tummy, with Mom making this high–pitched, scratchy scream. I shook her to try to get her attention and stop the yelling. I wanted her to help me just once. I told her to take the soap and clean her "privates."

With thanks to God, Mom took the soap and cleaned herself there. I was starting to see the light at the end of the tunnel. Now the main event ... I had to clean her bottom. There was no way she could do it. I reached out and asked for the soap that she help in her hand. I might add that my arm was starting to hurt from holding her up all this time. Mom just held the soap in her hand along her side, and I tried to take the soap from her.

As I reached for the soap, she dropped it in the water, and it began to do what soap does when dropped in the bathtub. It slid away toward the drain.

In the spirit of all the hours Mom taught me to dance and move to the performance of a song, I spun around so my back was now to the shower spigot and she was looking away. I was so proud of myself. Now all I had to do was reach down, pick up the bar of soap, and wash her derrière.

With my hand still around her waist, I went down on one knee, grabbed the soap, and began to wash her behind from the kneeling position. As if directed by Mel Brooks, mother released a blast of internal combustion with my face parallel to her hind quarter. There is no way to adequately describe that moment in my life.

There was nowhere to run. There was nothing to be said. Stevie just took one from Mom right in the face. Moments later, Bertha's bath time was over.

I hollered down to Tommy to bring me towels and a fresh nightgown. The way he avoided these kinds of events with Mother, I was thankful he heard me this one time. By this time Mom was showing fatigue and was no longer fighting me or saying much.

With all my sensitivity about touching my mother gone for the time being, I dried her off and managed to get a pink and green nightgown on her.

She finally cooperated, and we walked together back to her bedroom, where I sat her in her chair near the closet. I propped her up with a pillow and proceeded to strip her bed and put on clean sheets and blankets.

She gave me no problem getting her back into bed, and she smelled ever so clean. I, on the other hand, was soaking wet, disheveled, and exhausted. After tucking her in and putting up her protective side rails, I kissed her on the forehead and told her I loved her.

Turning out the light, I heard her say, "Thanks for helping me, Fanny."

Son's Rule: The love we hold for our parents is without boundaries. They can make us very angry and hurt our feelings during our relationships. Sometimes we may choose not to speak with Mom or Dad for a period of time just to get over the sting of something he or she might have said or done that hurt. However, what we learn from our walk as sons (and daughters) with parents with Alzheimer's/dementia is that there are no limits to our love. All that has gone before is but a prelude to the length and depth of loving care we will provide ... right on time.

Chapter 9

Bert Alert

Keeping Mom in her own home with my older brother, Tommy, was my mother's most strident demand. Early in the years following my father's death in 2002, Mom was still demonstrating good agility, probably thanks to her early life as a dancer, and although dementia was showing its first effects on her mind, we kept a fairly regular schedule. I didn't receive many telephone calls during the working day from Mom or Tommy, at least no more than what might be considered normal for family members.

By late 2003, November to be exact, I began getting telephone calls from Mom and Tommy that were directly linked to Mom's increasing hallucinations. These calls came so often that I began to refer to them as a "Bert Alert." (Bert was one of my mother's nicknames, Bokie the other.)

For reasons that I scarcely took time to consider, I resisted purchasing a cell phone for as long as I could. To me it was another thing that I would have to carry around, and besides, I never felt that any conversation was important enough that couldn't wait until I was sitting at home or in my office.

When mother became my responsibility I saw the "telecommunications light" and purchased a cell phone that was reminiscent of a Star Trek communicator, or at least that was the selling point I told myself. Suffice to say, if it was good enough for Captain Kirk, it was good enough for me.

I made it clear to family members, a few friends, and those associated with Mom's care not to call me on this device unless there was some urgency to communicate. Little did I know that in a matter of weeks, my mother and brother alone would call me like I was a line operator for a telethon.

When I purchased the phone in 2002, I was most insistent with the salesperson that I had to have a cell phone number that I could get my mother to memorize. I was trying to explain to the salesperson, a young lady in her early twenties, that due to mother's dementia I wanted to make it easy for her or my brother to call me in an emergency. I recall the conversation well because she had never heard of dementia and made the flip comment to me, and I quote, "Well, if they can't reach you, you can always call them."

Each day I would annoy my mother and brother by having them repeat my cell phone number over and over so they might memorize it, and more easily call me if the "need" occurred. Mother was never one to spend time on the telephone and totally balked at having a cell phone. She liked her kitchen table phone with the enlarged numbers with the perpetual coffee stain on the receiver.

As we got into 2004, mother was hallucinating daily with a variety of visions that leaped beyond the experiences and people of her life. These delusions worked overtime, late into the night, often keeping my brother awake in his own room. Tommy's delicate emotional state, especially after the death of our father, made him almost incapable of handling the chaotic content of Mom's machinations.

For the better part of Tommy's life, he could come to my mother at any time of day or night to talk to her, secure a needed hug, and just hear her quiet voice. Mom was the calming influence and steady hand for Tommy.

With Alzheimer's/dementia forever lurking and growing in its control of Mom's mind, he could not count on her hearing him or responding with the quiet reassuring demeanor that had marked Mom's interactions with Tommy.

As the hallucinations increased, so did the phone calls from Tommy, many in the early morning hours and each with Tommy in a highly emotional state. There was no saying no. Whether I was sitting down to dinner, or fast asleep, all it took was for Tommy to call, and I was in an instant state of "Bert Alert."

Even though in my professional and public life I found it rude for someone's cell phone to go off in the middle of a meeting or social function, I was guilty of keeping the ringer on for Mom and Tommy.

The Bert Alert was never ignored, although times I wished I could have not heard that distinctive ring. (By the way, after Mom died, I changed that ring tone. I never wanted to hear it again. I have heard that ring tone on other phones while out and about, and it still puts me in that instant state of Bert Alert—meaning go to Mom now.)

Of the hundreds of Bert Alerts that I logged, a few notables come to mind.

Sherbie Needs You

In June 2007, I was teaching my fifty young men in the Developing Tomorrow's Professionals program on the campus of Southern Connecticut State University. I had a strict rule that during our five-hour Academic Saturday class, all cell phones were to be turned off. I, of course, was about to break my own rule.

I was teaching a segment of study-skills training that addressed the importance of eliminating distractions in harnessing maximum learning capabilities. How ironic that Mom picked this day to evoke a masterpiece of distraction.

In the midst of my instructional thunder and metaphors, my cell phone, tucked in my leather briefcase, went off. It could only be Tommy or Mom. I was compelled to answer, despite the giggles and chuckles of my young men and their adult mentors who filled the room.

Making my apologies, I grabbed the phone and quickly stepped into the corridor.

Flipping the phone open, I hear, "Tommy, this is your mother."

Wishing to make this call as brief as possible, I respond, "Mom, this is Stevie, not Tommy. I can't stay on long. I'm in class."

Mom, never one to value my chosen profession even before dementia struck, said, "Stevie, this is your mother. You'll have to come over to the house now."

I must have rolled my eyes or shook my head awaiting the disposition of the crisis of the day. "Mom, what's the problem?"

"We have a problem with Sherbie [her cat]. Sherbie needs you."

"Mom, I can't stay on. What's the problem with the cat?"

"He hasn't pooped in three days. You need to get him to the vet."

"Mom, how do you know that?" (My brother cleaned the cat box every morning.)

"A mother can tell."

"Okay, I have to run. I'll be over after class."

I returned to class to issue another apology to the playful snickering of my young men who enjoyed the moment of Dr. Hoag's "distraction."

Getting back into the lesson as fast as I could, I returned to the issue of distractions with an explanation of "emotional deaf spots." The ring tone erupted yet again, piercing the tiered lecture hall as laughter abounded. To save some degree of "professional face," I decided to stand tall right in front of the class and answer the phone.

I decided to have the conversation with my mother for all the class to hear. Why I chose that course of action still baffles me, but it is still remembered by at least one person who was in attendance that morning.

I repeated everything Mom said to me during that call: "Yes, Mother. You're watching the cat, and *the cat* says *he* needs a doctor. Okay, I'll take him to the vet. Right, you know he's in pain. Mom, I need to go. I'll be there as soon as I can. Sherbie says thank you? Tell Sherbie, no problem. Bye, Mom."

Tommy Has a Little Girl under His Bed

One of the hallucinations Mom had was her belief that Tommy had a young girl hiding in the house and that Tommy wouldn't own up to it. This delusion with different twists went on for weeks.

There were a few parts and challenges to this saga. Mom was accusing Tommy of lying. By nature, Tommy is totally honest. He has never even attempted a lie or a deception. His mental and emotional problems are obvious to those around him, but tell a lie? He wouldn't know how.

It was mid-afternoon on a Wednesday and the cell phone rings at the office. Before answering I immediately feel my heart rate increase as a "Bert Alert" is about to commence. Candidly, I don't remember a single a call from mom or Tommy or even dad when he was alive just to say "hi." It was always a crisis, small or large, imagined or real.

The call from mom went like this:

"Stevie, stop what you're doing. Come over right now. The police might be on their way at any minute."

(My first thought was the word *police*! My self-instruction said … stay calm.) "Mom, did you call the police?"

"No, people know."

"Mom, tell me what's going on."

"Tommy is hiding a ten-year-old girl under the couch."

(I know a few things right away. This was a delusion of epic portion because it involved Tommy. Tommy must have been an emotional mess as a result of whatever she was saying to him about an imaginary girl.)

I said, "Momm tell me about the police. Did you call the police?"

"No, but they must be outside looking for the girl. You'd better get here before they arrest Tommy."

At this point I was more worried about Tommy. I traveled as fast as I could from Hartford to Wallingford. I went to Tommy's room, where I found him crying in his bed, telling me, "Mommy is crazy." He told me everything Mom was saying, and this led to a heart-to-heart conversation about dementia.

My fifty-five-year-old brother could not understand what was happening to his mommy. I sat with him for two hours trying my best to explain Alzheimer's/dementia, a disease that I didn't fully comprehend.

Nothing I said that day or in the future would make this easier on my brother. For today, I had to find a way to defuse this delusion. Once again I was about to apply pragmatism and logical thinking in attempting to reason with Mom. I would crash and burn, but it was memorable.

I went into her room, where she was half-asleep. My hope was that the "little girl" episode was gone and forgotten. I was wrong again. I sat on the side of her bed and startled her a little. She woke in an instant and started talking about Tommy and how he was hiding a ten-year-old girl under the couch.

I listened calmly and tried to explain that there was no little girl in the house. Mom bristled and told me to look under the living room couch. Beside the fact that the couch has three inch legs, I suggested she accompany me to the living room and look for the girl with me. Mom agreed. I figure, *Wow, I might actually talk her out of a hallucination.*

I helped her on with her robe and slippers, and down the short staircase we went to the dark living room. I set her down in the large recliner chair in the middle of the room. I hadn't turned on a light yet, and Mom started yelling, "She's under the couch. Right there. You can see her leg."

I turned on all the lights and the room was totally illuminated. I turned Mom's chair so it was pointed at the couch. Tommy stood on the stairs watching this whole scenario play out, so I felt a bit of pressure to bring it to some conclusion. Tommy was on the verge of really blowing up emotionally.

I moved the couch, and with little room to maneuver, I turned it over as gently as I could.

Mom barked out, "Look, there she is."

Tommy shouted, "Stevie, is that dementia?"

"Yes, Tommy," I responded.

My brother was now connecting the word dementia with the condition of his mother that he was seeing from across the room.

She continued talking, and I tried to participate. "Mom, I will open the door and let her out, so she can go back to her family, okay?"

Mom gave me the sourest of expressions and retorted, "She is going. She doesn't like you anyway. You are too homely. She likes Tommy."

With that, I opened the front door, and my mother waved good-bye—and you know what? I did too.

This "Bert Alert" was over. This young girl or another girl would show up again in different places around the house, and Tommy would call in a Bert Alert each time, no matter the time of day, but he never again was brought to tears as a result of Mother's visions.

Son's Rule: Alzheimer's/dementia connects you in some highly emotional ways to your mom or dad. You will always want to defuse or ease what appears to be a stressful moment in the midst their hallucination. Remember, the real stress is not on them but on you and all those who love them. We never get used to having our daily lives interrupted or upended by the calls for help from our Alzheimer's/dementia parents or other family members who share in the care for them, but we must try to keep our own feelings in check. If we allow ourselves to wear down emotionally or physically, or succumb to the daily pressures of caring for them, we won't be of full strength when they need us most.

Chapter 10

"What's My Name?"

As a teacher I have always emphasized the importance of one's name. In the Developing Tomorrow's Professionals program that I have been blessed to coordinate these last few years, we teach each young man the value of his name and require that he stand on his name when he prepares and submits his academic work. I have said to my young men so many times, "Let your name have meaning." It is paramount in the development of each young man (and woman) that he begins to recognize that by placing his name on a homework assignment or test, it represents the best he has to give and a maximum effort.

A person's name has power. Every person loves to hear someone else speak his or her name, whether through an introduction or connected with a positive moment. I contend that many young people allow their names to be amended, replaced, or prefixed because of dissatisfaction with themselves, or the preconceived opinion of friends (even family members) who give a nickname based on physical appearance or some childhood quirk. Names I have heard recently include Tink-Willy, Spike, Buba, Hen, Slick, and the always-flattering Fatty. Along the way, young people assume more the characteristics of those nicknames rather than the elegance and prestige of their legal given name.

Having been the object of a few nicknames from childhood through college that were not given to me for my beauty or intellect, it has always been important to me to be called by my name: Stephen, Steve, Dr. Hoag, etc.

Immediately following Mom's heart attack and stroke in 1999, I got the first taste of her not knowing who I was. The doctor who performed the quadruple bypass told me she might hallucinate after the surgery, but I was unprepared for her temporary loss of memory relative to my name and our relationship. After months of rehabilitation, she remembered who I was and I was thankful (and naïve) to believe I'd never have to go through that again.

At the onset of Mom's Alzheimer's/dementia, she would occasionally call me Tom(my brother's name), Joe (my father's name), or Sam (her brother's name; Sam died in 1947). As time went on I was identified as any number of different people, including former boyfriends, girlfriends, doctors, and a few big-band leaders from the 1940s.

During those initial meetings with Mom's doctors I learned that the loss of memory, especially with everyday items or the names of family members, is common with Alzheimer's.

Early in our Alzheimer's walk together, I didn't handle it all that well. When she called me by a name other than my own, or didn't know me at all, I would immediately correct her, sometimes rather sternly. After all, I rationalized, I fed her and bathed her, and I am her son. That's a pretty personal and intense relationship. How could she forget me and my name?

During this early period of my caring for Mom, I instituted a new phrase into my vocabulary that I would often say out loud when she pushed my patience to the various limits of endurance.

The phrase was *Patience Meter.* In keeping with the Alzheimer's physiognomies, the Patience Meter was an imaginary piece of technology that was strapped to my heart, indicating my level of patience that was just expended and the level of patience remaining before I turn into a babbling moron.

My most vivid recollection of this incorrect name calling occurred on Christmas day in 2002, taken directly from my journal entry of that day.

The discourse between Mom and me went as follows.

I handed mother a large Christmas gift, her first of many that year. The gift was a little over-wrapped, as I often did. Mom was sitting up very pretty and neat on the living room couch after her morning bath and her breakfast of cereal, fruit, and coffee. I sat across from her on this tiny little antique rocking chair so I could help with the wrappings if she needed assistance.

I handed the first Christmas gift to her.

"Thank you, Joe, this looks nice."

"Steve!"

"Joe, this is from Steve?"

"No, Mom, I'm Steve."

(The Patience Meter was switched on and operational.)

"Oh, it's from Joe? Thanks Joe."

"Mom ... Mom ... I'm Steve."

(The Patience Meter reaches 20 percent.)

(Mom was twelve inches away and calmly looking at me.) "Okay ... where's Tom?"

"Tom's in the kitchen."

"Oh okay. Joe, is Stevie coming over this morning?"

"Mom, I'm sitting in front of you."

"Joe, get me a scissors. I can't open my present."

(The <u>Patience Meter</u> soared to 50 percent and climbed.)

(I yanked the package from my mother to get her attention.) *"Mom, I'm Steve—Steve, your son. Mom!"*

(She grabbed the present back from me.) "Give me my present back. You open your own gift, Tommy."

(Tom heard his name and yelled out.) *"I'm in the kitchen having my breakfast!"*

"Good ... Joe, go wake up Tommy and let's have breakfast."

(Mom rose and walked to the kitchen.)

The Patience Meter maxed out. My joyful *I love you, Mom* Christmas morning, gift-opening plan crashed and burned like wrapping paper in the fireplace.

Son's Rule: Each of us has something we hold of great value. For some it is a possession such as a car, a house, jewelry, or expensive clothing. For others it is the manner of respect or attention family and friends show you. And then you might highly value your own name, or a few cherished experiences you have shared with a loved one. When a parent is afflicted with Alzheimer's/dementia things that used to be of value to them, or to you, are often turned upside down or inside out. Remember always the indefinable and unlimited *love* you hold in your heart for your mom or dad. That never changes. It is difficult at times to remember when so much instant emotion comes your way.

Just as you were, *and still are* to your mom or dad, you are their *treasure*. Look at your mom or dad as *your* treasure now. Just as if you discovered a treasure chest on a long-sunken ship in the middle of the ocean, you would overcome every obstacle to find, secure, and take care of that treasure.

For me the Holy Word speaks best to my mom, my treasure, in Luke 12:34: "For where your treasure is, there will your heart be also."

Chapter 11

Appointment with Yesterday

Mom's dementia advanced in 2004 and 2005 with almost overnight swiftness, altering her personality and behavior. I saw these changes more prominently once the sun set each day. I don't know if there is any medical reason why that occurred, but the evenings were certainly more packed with inexplicable behavior than the morning or afternoon hours.

On one particular day in April 2005 I became aware that the fabric of time and space might have encountered a "rip" as Mom drew me into a unique event. You must remember that during most years with Mom during the Alzheimer's/dementia period, I really tried to play along with almost every scenario her distorted memory created. If she identified me as someone she knew many years ago, I did my thespian best to make that person come alive again. I played her sisters, her parents, my own father, former teachers, her friends from elementary school, and my most challenging roles, her high school boyfriends. I learned very quickly that if she was convinced someone was in the room and I was identified as that person, there was no chance of talking her out of it, and believe me, I *tried*!

As stated, the late afternoons as the sun set were the most problematic for anyone who was with Mom. The delusions and subsequent loss of inhibitions resulted in her making some rather offensive sounds and almost instantly transitioning to an infinite number of locations and times in her life, or the life she thought she had lived.

Among her "fantasyland" expeditions were the moments when she would insist she had an appointment, an eminently arriving guest, or a date with an amorous mystery man. As the years passed I could almost see it coming and prepared to perform with the flexibility of Jonathan Winters or the innate dramatic acumen of Sir Lawrence Oliver.

This took more than a bit of getting used to, and I never did fling my arms around these moments. As a pragmatic man, my first inclination was to try to correct her first, suggesting she did *not* have an appointment. But applied pragmatism against the manifestations of dementia is a losing proposition, and I often came away a tad angry, frustrated, and intellectually drained, so I went along.

One of the first moments Mom and I shared with one of these "appointments with yesterday" came in April 2005. She wasn't at the stage yet where her steadiness of foot had diminished. Goodness, we were still dancing together from time to time.

I arrived at the house from my office in Hartford around five thirty, and upon closing the front door, Mom yelled out, "I'll be right down. Don't rush me. I need to put on a little makeup."

Now, I knew my mother's and brother's schedules better than I did my own, and I had no recollection of any reason why she would be applying makeup. It wasn't a Thursday, our regular food shopping night, so I had no idea what she had in mind.

Mom was from that wonderful generation where a woman would never consider going out in public for any reason without doing her hair (combing, bobby pins, barrettes, and a smidge of hairspray, or a dab of Dippity-do), brushing a touch of rouge on her cheeks and applying a light coating of red lipstick to her lips, followed by the unique exercise of biting down with the lips on a piece of tissue paper. I always thought this was a way for a woman not to appear too alluring, all the while leaving a good smudge of lipstick on the front teeth.

As I approached the stairs to her bedroom, she was hot-stepping it down the stairs and asking me to get her coat.

I asked the foolish question, "Mom, where are you going?"

She replied in a second, "I have an appointment with Dr. Boyd."

Astonished at this stage of the dementia game with just obvious logic kicking in at that moment, I told her Dr. Boyd had died many years ago. This was my usual first step. Be logical and try to talk her out of it.

"Don't be silly," she snapped back. "I just got off the phone with his nurse."

As I wasn't geared down from the day's work and had nothing on my evening's dance card, I decided to play along with this hallucinogenic engagement. *After all,* I thought, *the worst that happens is that we stop to get a little dinner.*

I wasn't sure where I was going to take her, or even that once I got her in the car, she would remember where we were going or why.

As we approached the car with her holding my arm as she always did, and rather tightly, I wondered if Dr. Boyd's former office was still there.

Dr. Boyd and his partner Dr. Ferguson were our family doctors in the 1950s and '60s, but it had been a long time since I'd visited their office. As I recalled, their office, located on South Main Street, was a converted two-family house.

Onward ... I helped her to the car, whereupon I opened the door for her and attempted to guide her into the front seat, whereupon she evoked one of her most popular expressions during the dementia days: *"Don't touch me. I don't need any help."*

"Stevie chivalry" is "dementia dismissed."

Once planted in the passenger seat with seatbelt affixed, off we went to her "appointment" with Dr. Boyd. By the way, Mom wouldn't let me help her with the seat belt, so the top of it was wrapped around her neck like a convict in the gallows. I did try.

My spontaneously designed plan was to drive to the address where Dr. Boyd's office used to be and just calmly show her that she must have just imagined the appointment. I held out hope that a visual would turn on the light on her memory and the aberration would be dead on arrival.

I pulled in front of the location and prepared to show her the error in her thinking. I stopped the car, unhooked her seat belt, and prepared to take her to the porch in front of the house to show her Dr. Boyd was no longer a doctor in residence. Before I could utter a few kind words to soften the impact, out the door she went.

Scooting around to escort her up the stairs, Mom had already navigated the three small stairs at the front of the office.

Trailing her, concerned that she was moving too fast and a trip or fall was possible, she reached the front door. Rather than knock or ring the doorbell, she immediately tried to open the door to the house she still believed to be Dr. Boyd's office.

Whew, the door was locked. So Mom looked for the doorbell to announce her arrival. It now occurred to me that there was about to be other players in this little drama ... anyone who walked by and anyone who might answer the door.

With Mom applying heavy pressure with her thumb to the doorbell, a man came to the door and asked how he might help us. I tried to spit out a sentence such as, "Sorry to bother you; we must have come to the wrong address."

Mom, never last with a word or a song, beat me to the response, answering the gentleman, "I have an appointment with Dr. Boyd." To accent the moment, Mother engaged in an act of flatulence. It was bold in countenance, but to her credit she issued an instant "excuse me."

Now looking at me with a cocked, quizzical head, like a dog when it hears a foreign sound, the man in the doorway said, "I'm sorry, but there's no Dr. Boyd here."

Expecting that this response would end this little adventure, Mom responded, "Dr. Ferguson, I recognized you right away. I have a four o'clock appointment with Dr. Boyd. Would you like to see me instead of him?"

At the same moment she was saying these words to the totally puzzled inhabitant, she grabbed the door handle and tried to enter.

Now, the gentleman seemed to be taking on a bit of anxiety with this situation, and with a gesture of hand, he denied Mom entrance.

Never one to accept a rejection, Mom began her doctor-patient predisposition right there on the porch.

With events happening faster than I can either respond to or believe, she said, "Dr. Ferguson, I've had this terrible irritation above my ribs."

The man is actually standing behind the door in quiet disbelief, seemingly just to see this thing play out, and unsmilingly says, "I know. I just heard it."

I finally opened my mouth and, smiling broadly, told the gentleman to forgive the intrusion and we'd just go look for Dr. Boyd elsewhere.

Mother turned to me with malice in her eyes and told me to be quiet and let her discuss her problem with Dr. Ferguson.

The gentleman had probably reached his "good-guy" limit, and before he shut the door with some measure of finality, he said with sarcasm of forethought, "I hope you find that doctor and soon."

As it happened sometimes, although not often enough, some of these visions and hallucinations Mom experienced ended abruptly, and she had no recollection it ever occurred.

With hastened steps we returned to the car, and I drove her home with nary a word between us, hopeful that this event would leave her thoughts and that I would find some understanding in time. All was going well as we pulled up under the carport with no mention of this visit to see doctors Boyd and Ferguson.

Entering the house with brother, Tommy, playing the television loudly as usual, I helped Mom over the high step to the kitchen from the carport. She immediately sat down at the kitchen table as I helped her off with her coat. *So far, so good,* I was thinking. *She hasn't said a word. Yet!*

All was going so well. Then Tommy yelled out from the living room, "What did Dr. Boyd say about your rash?"

There's momentary silence, and then Mom said to me, "Give me Dr. Boyd's telephone number. I need to ask him about this rash above my ribcage."

Son's Rule: As the sun goes down each day, you may find an increased level of illusions, delusions, and flat-out fantasyland moments. Most of these delusions won't last all that long, whether you acknowledge them and play along or just choose to ignore them like they aren't really there—which they aren't. However, there are some delusions that just keep giving.

Chapter 12

Schtooped

Mother never applied any form or fashion of corporal punishment to me or my brother. This was due in large part because my father was a rather violent man who hit us for the smallest of infractions. As I entered my teens I began to have little emotional outbursts, questioning longstanding family rules and assigned chores. In typical teenage, post-pubescent discourse I would question many longstanding rules. "Why is it always me? Why doesn't Dad to it? Why don't you hire someone to do it?"

Now, I had enough control to *never* question anything around my father. If he was in the house, you kept your mouth closed. Dad's number-one rule was, "Don't speak unless you are spoken to." We learned early to walk and talk in silence around him.

With Mom, I could let loose and express myself. She was my best friend. She always listened and forgave my occasional displays of rebellion, providing I refrained from cursing. Growing up I never had a large circle of friends, and I thanked her repeatedly for being my confidant.

One of the standards I maintained in the evolving relationship with Mom from my post-high school to adult years was never to use foul language around her—not that I was an aficionado of profanity anyway in any circumstance.

There was one incident in my life in 1962 that would come full circle in 2007 that Alzheimer's/Dementia made possible. It was not the happiest of moments but one that showed that

Mom, despite the consequences of the disease, was still right with us.

Mom was brought up in a small three-bedroom farm on the edge of Fitchburg, Massachusetts, with her eight sisters and one brother. Being the second youngest of the nine siblings, Mom's childhood was one of constant activity and was rich in the memories of her sisters and all their many friends and beaus. When Mom got together with her closest sister, Fanny (Florence), the conversation always got around to the friends they had growing up and the boyfriends who hovered around the more popular, attractive sisters in the family, especially Evelyn and Dorothy.

Despite all the aunts on my mother's side and the uncles on my father's side, we didn't visit them much and they sure didn't visit us in Connecticut, except for my aunt Fanny and her husband, John. I was always fascinated with the way Mom acted when she was with Fanny. She was like a different person. In our usually tense home environment, Mom didn't smile or laugh much, but when Fanny came to visit or we visited her, Mom cackled and smiled almost constantly. As a boy growing up, I wanted to be close to all this smiling business, so I would do anything to get close to their banter. I loved to listen in on adult conversation. I never did fully understand why, but I was always drawn to older people talking with one another.

Actually, I didn't always understand what Mom and Aunt Fanny were talking about as they often spoke in Yiddish, a form of Hebrew slang. I was often shooed away, but I usually found a way to sneak back to within earshot of the conversation.

One of my favorite ploys was to pocket Aunt Fanny's cigarette lighter. She smoked Lucky Strike cigarettes. They were short little filter-less "cigs," as she called them. She never lit them with a match.

I never knew why, but as far back as I can remember, I always liked to light her cigarettes and she let me. That simple act of flicking the button at the top of the lighter and holding the flame for Aunt Fanny to "light up" made me feel special somehow.

To ensure that Aunt Fanny would ask me to light her "cig," I would pocket the little gold lighter. I wouldn't let anyone see me hide it. When Aunt Fanny looked for her lighter and asked everyone in the room if they had seen it, I instantly volunteered to look for it. After a few minutes of faking like I was looking between cushions or under magazines, I would produce the lighter and offer to light her cig. Usually this would gain me a closer seat to listen in on their schoolgirl banter. By the way, my favorite place to hide her lighter was in my sock, just inside my sneaker.

I just loved watching Mom so happy in her conversations with Aunt Fanny. I learned all about my aunts and their love interests (although I didn't really understand it all at the time).

I even learned a word that got me into trouble when I was eleven years old.

Mom and Fanny would use the word *schtoop* from time to time. Now, I didn't know what that word meant, but it always seemed to precede the pronouns "him" or "her." I was learning about grammar in school, so I had the pronoun thing down pretty well. Every so often in their conversation, it was "He schtooped her," or "She was schtooped," or the question variation, "She got schtooped?"

I was starting to understand that "schtooped" meant something *bad* happened, like a mistake on a math paper. In my eleven-year-old vernacular, this might be stated as "I schtooped problem seven." I think I had pretty well figured it out, and on a spring day in 1962, I discovered that I had schtooped really bad.

We were visiting Aunt Fanny and Uncle John. Dad, Uncle John, Aunt Fanny, and Mom were all watching the Boston Red Sox game on their big black and white television (must have been a twenty-inch screen). In one of those rare instances we were allowed to sit on the floor and watch the game with the adults. Mom and Aunt Fannie were talking it up as usual, hardly paying any attention to the game. Even though I loved baseball, I enjoyed listening to Mom and Aunt Fannie more. Dad was getting annoyed that he couldn't concentrate on the game with all the talk going on in the room and asked them to "pipe down" (a "Dad expression" I still cannot define).

Mom and Aunt Fannie stopped talking as ordered, and all the focus was on the baseball game. With all eyes on the television, the Red Sox shortstop, Eddie Bressoud (amazing how you remember details like that), threw a ball errantly, allowing a run to score.

Dad and Uncle John threw their hands up, and Dad yelled, "C'mon Broussoud."

Sitting with adults watching a game, an uncommon thing for me at that time, I chimed in, "He schtooped it."

From somewhere in the room, some power (Dad) belted me in the back of the head, followed by one head-turning slap to my left cheek. Lifted by the back of my shirt and trousers, I found myself on Dad's lap being spanked in front of everyone.

I saw Mom's expression from the other side of the room, and she immediately raised her fingers to her lips to shush me, which meant "don't cry." There was no crying. My brother and I learned through repetitive training that crying extends the beating, so we had to grin and bear it, so to speak.

After the spanking I was yanked up by Dad and pushed from the room. Mom followed me out, taking me to the little pantry near the kitchen. She explained to me quietly that "schtoop" was a bad word and I should never have said it. I asked my mother what the word meant. I reminded her that she and Aunt Fannie used it all the time. Mother would not tell me the definition of the word, only that it was a very bad word to be used only by adults. I was confined to the pantry for an hour or so and I thought about what had happened. I then realized I had been "schtooped."

Fast forward forty-five years! I was sitting across from Mom at the kitchen table, watching her enjoy a frozen dinner that she had selected from the freezer. Sherbie, the cat, sat poised by her coffee cup, waited for Mom to extend a fingertip covered in the chicken broth from the dinner.

I was trying to engage mother in conversation. No matter what I said, she would look at me and just ignore my questions and keep eating. It was sunset time, and I knew the delusions of dementia would be at full strength. By conversation I had hoped to keep Mom's mind occupied and minimize the fantasy world.

After twenty minutes of being overlooked, I moved over to a seat right beside her at the table. Showing my aggravation, I took the fork from her hand, got right in her face, and said, "Mom, talk with me."

Mom just looked at me, took her fork back, and started to eat again.

Shaking my head in apparent defeat, I casually say, "I'm schtooped."

With stealth and unanticipated suddenness, *I was slapped in the face.* My head turned, not believing my mother, who has never lifted a hand in anger to me, just slapped me.

Looking most shocked, I asked her, "What was that for?"

Without hesitating she responded, "You do not use that word. Didn't you learn your lesson?"

With my mouth open in disbelief, I thought, *What lesson is she talking about?* Turning my head toward the table to consider what that lesson might have been, it dawned on me. No way could Mom remember that event from 1962. My eyes snapped back to her and I asked, "You can't remember my name or what day of the week it is, but you remember that time when Dad spanked me for saying *schtooped?*"

Again, she corrected me and told me not to say that word. I promised not to say it again. I got up from the table, talking to myself. How could this remote event from forty-five years ago remain pristine in her brain when so many memories of significance might be lost due to Alzheimer's/dementia?

Son's Rule: Your mom (or dad) with Alzheimer's/Dementia might appear to have lost a high percentage of her memory. Mom might not respond in the manner she used to, relative to her longstanding habits and rules of conduct. She might not enjoy the same foods or "oooh and ahhh" at the lighting of the Christmas tree or smile at the sight of the grandchildren or great-children. Your parent may appear docile or not listening when engaged in conversation, but never forget that pieces of memories, past practices, and rules of conduct may have endured the damages of dementia. Should you take it for granted Mom doesn't remember or won't respond to stimulus as she once did, you might find yourself in for a wonderful surprise of memory recollection ... on the receiving end of a pointed rebuke or right cross.

Chapter 13

The Gold Shoes

Mother was never one to spend a lot of time shopping for clothes. She was raised in humble circumstances on a small farm in Fitchburg, Massachusetts, one of eight sisters. As she often explained, each sister took good care of the few garments she wore because all of their clothing would be handed down to the next youngest sister. Even when all the sisters were married adults, they still shared each other's clothes, including outerwear and shoes. As one sister died, her clothing was often passed along to the other sisters. What made it easy was that they were all about the same size.

During my childhood, if Mom and Dad had to go somewhere special like a wedding or a bowling banquet, Mom would check with my aunt Fannie for something to wear. Actually, Mom always had a good eye for color and what coordinated well in an outfit. Mom was hardly a flashy dresser by any means, but she was no matronly woman either. To the point, Mom always looked good and well put together in her outfits. Notably, she had accumulated a wide assortment of shoes of many colors and styles (all previously worn) from her sisters. She never went out without makeup, and wherever she went with Dad, she wore a dress with an assortment of costume jewelry at her disposal (another hand-me-down).

Thursday night food shopping with Dad included her "dolling" up a bit, as she called it. When symptoms of Alzheimer's/dementia began, her ability to discern a logically constructed outfit started to show signs of the *bizarre*.

I had learned that people with this affliction would sometimes behave inappropriately in public, but like many aspects of disease I was not prepared for the time when my mother's attire went from "tastefully conservative" to "gypsy woman."

Like many women and some men (such as myself), shoes are an important component of one's attire, and the most time-intensive decision Mom would make getting dressed was in her choice of shoes. The bottom of the closet she shared with my father in their ten-foot square bedroom was filled with her shoes, and while most of these shoes were adult hand-me-downs from her sisters who had previously passed away, they spanned about fifty years of shoe fashions and styles.

When Dad and Mom ventured out to routine food shopping or attending events at the senior citizens' center, one thing you could count on was that Mom would wear shoes appropriate to her dress in color.

After Dad died and Mom's care passed to me, I found myself helping her dress. In 2002 this was nothing more than helping her find a particular dress or locating some ancient pair of shoes in the closet. As each month passed and Alzheimer's/dementia increased its hold, I began to actually dress her ... *and* do her makeup. None of these functions were done without varying degrees of resistance from Mom. She needed my help but fought like crazy to hang on to her dignity and self-reliance. (These weren't functions I wanted to do either, but dressing Mom was mild compared to the other tasks I would eventually perform [as covered in other chapters].)

After Dad passed, I assumed the responsibility of taking Mom anywhere and whenever she wished to go. Departure time for these often extemporaneous jaunts began when she was dressed and never at the prearranged time. To be sure, Mom's sense of time due to Alzheimer's was not the stuff of the United States Naval Observatory.

Mom never put on her shoes until she was ready to leave the house. As her shoes were always the last thing she put on, even after pulling on an overcoat or jacket, I often helped her put them on. I asserted myself as a matter of safety, but more as a matter of expedience. She could linger, and putting on each shoe could take thirty minutes.

Not being a big lover of feet to begin with, it wasn't the most enjoyable of tasks. By 2004, Mom's sense of color coordination for the choice of her outfits had become the makings of an Impressionist painting. The incongruous selection of shoes to occasion or shoe color to clothing color placed me in a state of constant eye-rolling. I probably muttered a few under-my-breath comments as I buckled, wrapped, shoe-horned, or laced the shoes on, but by and large, I just put them on her feet and out the door we went.

One of the more notable shoe events occurred on our regular trips to Stop & Shop on Thursday evening. On this memorable day, she wore white stretch pants, a red-white-and-blue pullover, and gold, strappy three-inch heels. The shoes were once owned by my late aunt Fanny, who got them from late Aunt Dora, so they had an easy thirty-five years on them and it showed.

The buckle on the left shoe was minus the little pin that goes through one of the holes on the strap to hold the shoe on her foot. This was no factor in Mom's selection. She instructed me to push a safety pin from the buckle side into one of the tiny holes on the strap. Easy enough, right? Unfortunately, the safety pin was cutting into the side of her foot, compelling her to tell me I was doing it wrong.

I explained as calmly as possible that the shoe as not designed for safety-pin repairs. She insisted this was the way she had done it before, but I never remembered her or anyone using a safety pin to keep a strappy high-heel shoe in place.

After numerous tries I could not position the safety pin from buckle to strap without the pin cutting into Mom's foot. I suggested she choose another pair of shoes. "*Nooooo*," she screamed at me, "I am wearing these shoes."

This was one of those moments of dementia-frustration for me. I thought, *I can't lose my temper, my cool, my rationale, my good judgment ... now can I?* You bet your life I could! The Patience Meter was on red alert.

With the sly playfulness of Shakespeare's Puck (a role I once performed), I decided to repair the shoe with something adhesive. I quickly ran up the stairs to mom's bedroom, grabbing the roll of masking tape that we used to keep her bed pads in place.

Rushing back down the stairs before she did something like bending over to try to fix the shoe herself, whereupon she would have taken a header, I saw her talking to the cat. Thanking God for the cat at that moment for keeping her distracted, I began my act of desperation.

Kneeling before her with tape in hand, I taped over the buckle to the strap as tightly as I could. Calling me a name that was not my own, Mom told me this will not keep the shoe on her foot and insisted I try something else. With the Patience Meter reading "*danger!*," I grabbed her foot with the shoe held in place with my hand and wrapped the masking tape around her foot and shoe. I applied the masking tape with the speed of an athletic trainer with the belief that when she saw the hideous appearance of the gold shoe wrapped in beige-colored tape, she would instantly decide to wear some other pair of shoes.

Frankly, I felt so good with this act of spontaneous frustration that I kept wrapping her foot and shoe with the masking tape until the roll was almost empty.

Ripping off the end piece of the tape and then patting her foot for good measure, I sarcastically proclaimed, "How's that, Mom?"

Expecting her full fury, she turned the emotional table on me and said, "*Good!* Let's go!"

Now the question is, do I let my mother be seen with a masking-taped-on shoe at Stop & Shop or demand that she wear another pair? Quickly considering all the consequences, the humiliation, the embarrassment, I conclude, "Absolutely— let's go food shopping."

From almost the day Dad died, Mom and I shopped each Thursday at Stop & Shop. There was an endless array of unique moments we shared between the aisles, pushing the shopping cart, but few had the preliminary drama of that day with the gold shoe. I must add that no word was spoken about the shoe during that day, but I did have to cut it off with scissors at bedtime.

Son's Rule: I learned early in my years of caring for Mom that Alzheimer's/dementia generates new levels of stubbornness. If you think your mother was rigid in her attitude before Alzheimer's/dementia reared its ugly head, stand by to abandon ship; you haven't seen donkey-obstinacy to match this level of pigheadedness. Try to remember—this will be funny someday.

Chapter 14

The Little Room ... *Where Memories Were Stored*

No matter the logic of inevitability or the planning for the future that most people do as they move along in life, there was nothing I could have done to prepare for the suddenness of our lives being altered when Dad died. I have often thought of what I might have done to prepare for these responsibilities. Each time I do, I recall all the conversations I had with Mom and Dad relative to what each wanted me to do when either one, or both of them, died.

For years I asked to see their wills. I enquired about their insurance policies and plans they had put in place for Tommy. Each time I brought it up I got a similar response. Their words always included something akin to, "Why so nosey? You looking for something for yourself? You think we can't take care of our own affairs?"

They made me feel downright awful anytime I asked about the future when all I wanted to do was have a plan. Friends of mine with parents of the same generation as mine seemed to know exactly what to do when their parents passed away. I could not find the words to motivate my aging parents to share any information.

When the moment of a life truth occurred—Dad's death— Mom had no idea where their will was located, and with the first signs of Alzheimer's showing, she wondered if there ever was a will. There was no personal file or any system of record keeping of any kind for either of them.

Here I was with a dead father and a mother didn't know if there was any life insurance. To make matters worse she evoked a new rule that would be one of her "battle cries" as we began to share the *Adventures in Alzheimer's/dementia-land* era. The new rule was "don't touch my things," and she started yelling this phase daily.

Here were some of the things mom expressly told me *not* to touch. I can hear her saying these phases now.

"Stay out of my dresser."

"Don't open my closet."

"Keep out of my cardboard boxes."

"Don't you open my mail."

And the depth of dogma with this new rule: "You can look at everything after I die."

With Dad's passing, and his end-of-life tasks to be done, I had to deal with challenges on multiple fronts. I remember a late-evening moment where I wrote a spin on Tennyson's words in my journal on June 28, 2003: "Funeral home to left of me, no records to the right of me, Tommy's emotional needs right in front of me," and mother was firing a verbal cannonade at me to the tune of the 1812 Overture with the words, *"Don't touch my things."*

It is important to note that at this particular time I was just getting used to the idea that Mother was exhibiting symptoms of Alzheimer's disease. Dad talked a lot to me, especially in the last year of his life, but he never mentioned anything concerning her health. Looking back, I don't think he had a clue that Mom had anything amiss health wise.

When mom entered her mid seventies, she started to ramp up behaviors that I considered annoying or contentious. I never heard her say a cross word to Tommy or Dad, but she always found reason to be critical or dismissive with me. I rationalized her behavior as transferred aggression or her continued disappointment with my choice of a career.

When the time came to ferret out information for probate that included taxes, mortgage, health insurance, banks accounts, and family members' addresses, mom stonewalled my every attempt.

I tried to provide every ounce of patience and understanding. I consulted doctors and homecare professionals to give me any insight possible into gaining the cooperation of my mother. It was a troubling time to be sure. Mom never really grieved Dad, at least not visually. She never shed a tear (that I saw), from the moment I told her of his death through the private funeral. Mom didn't talk about him or ever say she missed him. I suppose she had plenty of reasons to put him aside in her heart, but after all, they *were* married for fifty-two years.

Mom was as loving to Tommy and my daughters (her granddaughters) as ever. She constantly engaged Tommy in conversation and made him his meals. For her "other son, Stevie," she could be a verbal gunslinger.

As I began my new responsibilities with her, I tried to laugh off her barbs and tried not to bite the bait of her sarcasm or time-honored phrases such as "You were talented. You could have been someone," or "You could have brought me such 'nachas'" (Yiddish word meaning joy or pride a parent gets from her children).

In 2002 at age eighty-eight, Mom still wrote the checks to pay the bills, but she would never willingly let me see the bills or her checkbook that she kept hidden somewhere in her closet. I respected that privacy and her long-established authority, but Dad's passing brought me to a reality that she probably didn't have another eighty-eight years left. I had to find some sort of paper trail to wrap my arms around my tasks.

Of all the places in Mom's house where the needed information might be, the "little room," might just be it. The "little room," as my parents referred to it, was a tiny room perpendicular to their bedroom that was too small for a bedroom and just a fraction above the size of a walk-in closet. Growing up, this room was off limits to Tommy and me. We had seen this tiny room with the door open once in a while, and it was filled with stacks of pictures, old clothes and dolls, and an ancient roll-top desk, bulging at the seams with letters, newspaper clippings, and greeting cards. I called it the junk room and honored my parents' wishes and stayed out of there.

As the days passed and summer turned to fall in 2002, the pressure to uncover the information about Dad, Mom, and Tommy mounted. On more than a few occasions I entered the "little room," only to be rebuked by mom to "Get out of there … don't touch my things." The little-room door was almost touching the door to my mother's room, so the sheer geography made it almost impossible to gain entrance without her hearing or seeing me. Adding to the location problem was that the floor of the little room was covered with falling-apart cardboard boxes, sheet music, pictures, show programs, and personal letters wrapped in elastic-banded bundles. The room was at the very least a fire trap, but I was becoming more convinced that it held many answers. What I didn't know was that it also contained many answers to questions about Mom, Dad—and Tommy.

On a Sunday afternoon in mid November, I could wait no longer. I had to find such things as birth and marriage certificates, Dad's military discharge papers, insurance policies, and their will. Respect for my mother's wishes and personal property would have to be suspended, but I couldn't have her screaming at me for hours, risking a heart attack or the potential for her to call the police to have me arrested (see Chapter 7, The Case of the Stolen Wineglasses).

My solution? A ruse, a fabrication, a bald-faced lie to get my mother to let me go through the room. I told her we'd received a telephone call from the fire department and that they'd declared the house a fire threat and would be sending over a group of five firemen to inspect all the rooms in the house if we did not clear away all potential hazards.

The first half of the ruse didn't work, but the idea of strangers going through her bedroom, the cellar, and the "little room" scared the *crap* out of her.

With the seed of being overrun by men in red suits deeply planted in her brain, and with the vestiges of Alzheimer's/dementia beginning to impact her thinking, she agree to clean the "little room" with me. There was a catch. She told me she was in charge and I was not allowed to touch anything or take anything without her approval. I easily agreed to that stipulation. *I was finally in!*

After breakfast the following Sunday, with Mom fresh and clean, dressed in a light-blue warm-up suit that I bought for her some months ago, she opened to the door to the "little room." She wasted no time giving the orders with her common command, "Don't rush me."

Mom was not in a happy mood by any means, muttering under her breath all types of complaints and criticisms of me. There were no chairs in the room and no room for chairs. The floor was completely covered with loose papers, and there was but one lamp—a 1950s style, hooded, gooseneck lamp with tarnished metal and a shade that was dented and brown from age—in the dark room. This lamp used to occupy a corner of our living room. Now it was a relic of long-ago days, as was everything in here.

Mother asked me to turn on the light, and reaching over the almost-collapsing card table that stood just in front of the lamp, I twisted the little on/off switch. The light came on, but the knob broke in my fingers. Now illuminated, my eyes darted to every corner of the room, trying to see any box or container that might suggest "important documents." It was the most chaotic dumping ground for all things paper I had ever seen.

Mom held on to some rather dubious pieces of furniture for balance as she took her initial steps into the "little room," and I did my best to guide her, but she would have none of it. She pushed past a cardboard box with the contents overflowing, and holding on to the overloaded card table, she started to kneel. I went to grab her for safety and she pushed my hand away, saying, "I can do this myself." The question was, do what herself?

With that, Mom plopped down in the middle of the room, sitting upon a layer of old greeting cards, sheet music, and photographs. There was almost no place else to sit, so I carefully stepped around her and sat under a makeshift metal table that was heaped with small cigar boxes.

I suggested we go through all this stuff in an organized fashion, putting categories of materials in plastic bags, so we might go back at a later date and carefully inspect everything.

Mom was having none of that and told me we had to do it her way.

With the Patience Meter already turned on, I asked her how she proposed to go through everything and get organized. Spurning the word "organization," she told me to be quiet and let her go through the things she wanted to look at. Mom's mood was one of stern, almost mean-spirited indignation, making me feel most uncomfortable. She told me she didn't like being forced to clean because the firemen wanted her to. The ruse might just backfire.

Mom asked me to hand her one of the cigar boxes just above my head on the desk top. As I did, the box opened, and all sorts of black and white pictures spilled out all over my lap.

Mom randomly picked up the first photo. She stared at it for a few seconds and then kissed it, saying, *"Paaaaaaaaaaaaaaaa."* It was a photo of her father. She did not take her eyes from that edge-worn picture for a few minutes.

Now I was getting concerned. Mom held out her hand for another picture. Taking another from the same box, I handed it to her and she began to smile. That was always a good thing when Mother smiled.

I asked her who was in the picture, and once again the only word she uttered softly was, "Paaaaaaaaaaaaaaaaaaa."

One after another, each picture in the box was of her father, who'd died in 1930. The story of his death had been told to me countless times by my mother. In brief, it was her sixteenth birthday, December 23, 1930. Her father, Max Bever, had told Mom he would walk over to the theatre where she worked after school as a ticket taker and take her to dinner at a nearby diner. Mom saw her father approach from the other side of the street and waited for "Paaaaaa" to cross the street to her. Max (my grandfather) collapsed in the middle of the road, dying from a massive heart attack. On Mom's sixteenth birthday ...

As Mom looked at the photos of her father, not speaking any word, but "Paaaaaaaa," I wondered if that moment was on her mind.

From that instant on, I knew any hope of finding important legal documents on this day was probably lost.

Mom sat on the floor in the "little room" for three hours. I handed her one old picture at a time. She cupped each photo in her hands as though each one was newborn baby chick. She kissed many of them and at others she just shook her head. I would periodically ask her who was in the photo, but she said the names so softly I could only clearly hear a few like Henry, Adeline, Murray, and Tillie.

Mom was clearly lost in a long-ago time with long-since-departed family members and friends.

I could not determine if I was happy or sad for her. Mom wasn't ever tearful, surprised, and joyful or said more than a few words to me in those three hours. She didn't look at a photo and stack it neatly on the floor; rather, she looked at each picture, studying it, and when she was done, she just dropped it on the floor.

Wherever her heart and mind were in this exercise of photographic nostalgia I will never know or even venture a guess. She took so long to study a single picture, I wondered if she was struggling to remember who it might be and why she should remember the person.

I sat no more than three feet from her and watched as carefully as I have ever observed another human being. I wanted to know what she was thinking. The Alzheimer's/dementia had taken so much from her already, and that fact almost brought me to tears a few times that morning. Once in a while she would look up at me as if to ask, "Help me remember," but she didn't speak. Mom asked me to get her a glass of water, which I dutifully did.

When I returned with the water, she was clutching a photo against her heart.

"Who is that?" I enquired. Then I asked if I could see the picture.

She handed it to me, stating, "It's my sister Dora."

I looked at the picture of the small child with a white cowboy hat and realized it was me.

All at once I felt sorry for my mom. The often cantankerous Bertha was breaking my heart. I think she wanted to recognize every person in every picture and believed she had identified them all correctly. Although her heart recognized every person she saw on the worn paper, her brain twisted and turned her vision until she saw whomever she wanted to see at that moment.

I had forgotten all about the documents I needed to find. In those three hours, I let my heart celebrate the life and memories of my mother. It was the most perfectly calm, emotional hours of my life. My eyes watched her eyes. My heart beat for her heart. For that brief time on the floor in the "little room," Mom revisited a hundred people with a cascade of endless memories.

There would be another day for legalities and organization.

Son's Rule: Alzheimer's/dementia takes away what we know as the normal order of memory translation to feeling, specifically love, but it doesn't stop the parent's heart from reaching out to other places within his or her being to see what needs to be seen.

Remember, if your parent looks at you and doesn't seem to know you, there's a good chance that whoever Mom or Dad recognizes is someone he or she wants to see right now. Celebrate that it is you who is their conduit to joy.

Chapter 15

I Can Talk for Myself ... *the Oldest Living Call Girl*

Observing my parents over my lifetime brought about a basic conclusion. Mother was an intelligent woman, but she worked overtime to keep it cloaked from most of the world. My father on the other hand worked hard to make people believe he was smarter than he was. Mom kept her intellect tucked away so Dad would never feel not in control or inadequate in any way. She never wanted my father to feel stupid, diminished, or inferior. Dad purportedly finished eighth grade, but there is evidence to the contrary. My father's lack of education was a sore spot for him, and he never handled any type of criticism or failure very well.

Following my father's retirement after more than thirty years working in a factory, he and Mom would frequent the local senior citizens' center. There they would play cards or Dad played pool with the other senior men. At the age of seventy-four dad got into a fist fight with a man he was playing pool with because the man called him a dummy. When they played cards in various games like pitch, setback, or gin rummy, Mom would always seem to lose and Dad usually won.

The reason he won and Mom didn't was because she always threw him good cards. Mom just wanted to keep his ego up there on high, and she usually succeeded. Not surprisingly, Dad never knew she was doing it, and she relished the fact that he didn't figure it out. Having played a lot of cards with them, I can attest to Mother's skill at making it look like she didn't know what she was doing as a card player. When she wanted, she could dazzle with a deck of cards.

This low-key, rarely smiling mother of mine was the victim of physical abuse by my dad on numerous occasions during my childhood. God knows how many other times he might have hit her when I wasn't present. She left my dad twice that I remember, but I never heard her say a single harsh word to or about him at any time. She never showed any signs of temper or fear, and the only time I saw her cry was when my aunt Fanny died. This was a remarkably strong woman who I only came to fully appreciate as I began to take care of her.

Mom remained humble and understated in every part of her life. Dad did all the talking when company would come around, and even though a lot of what dad said was 100 percent blarney (the Irish term for lies and exaggeration), Mom never rolled her eyes or corrected him in any way. I often asked her why she never spoke when people were over, and she told me, "Your father has a lot to say, and I don't interrupt him."

With the onset of Alzheimer's disease, this woman of few words would become a woman of indescribable candor and verbosity. This modification in her personality brought about some events that can only be classified as *shocking*. Almost overnight the mother I knew who was quietly reserved morphed into a demonstrative, self-assured, outspoken, cantankerous woman of the world.

Perhaps the best illustration of the personality change was an event in 2006. Mom had been experiencing some hallucinations that had her talking long into the night with imagined parties in Boston and dates with Ralphie (Chapter 16 addresses her beau, Ralphie).

One evening around eight p.m., with the protective rails firmly in place around her bed because she couldn't get out without assistance, Mother was engaging in a loud rant that was driving Tommy berserk. I was announcing a high school basketball game that night, and Tommy called me by cell phone to tell me he heard a loud bang in Mommy's bedroom. I had been called many times before, so I knew a "Bert Alert" from Tommy. I called my daughter Kathleen on the way to Mom's house, feeling I might need an assist if this situation was bad.

Rushing to get there, I prayed Mom had not broken any bones, if in fact she did fall out of bed. I could not imagine how she could have gotten out of her bed since we installed high protective rails on the sides to prevent an accident.

I dashed up the stairs and into her bedroom. Flicking on the lamp on her night table, I didn't see Mom. The guard rails were in place, but no Mom.

Right on cue, mom calls out, "Teddy, you are sooooo funny!"

Moving around to the other side of her bed, mother is half-propped up with her back against the night stand, talking to someone named "Teddy."

I yell out, "Mom, are you all right?" as I knelt next to her. I saw blood on the floor and on her face and she is hysterical— with *laughter.* Mom is having this fast-moving conversation with someone called Teddy who apparently is making her belly laugh, causing her to make this cackling laugh that I had never heard before. If I didn't know that Mom never touched booze or even a beer, I could have sworn she was drunk. The convolution of what was real and unreal was scaring me now as I started to look for cuts and other injuries.

I yelled down to Tommy to get me some towels. I wanted to wipe the blood from Mom's face and try to get her back to "camp reality." My mother continued her conversation with Teddy, which was filled with references to things like "sand in my suit" and "bugs in my hair."

Holding Mom in my right arm I proceeded to clean her face of the blood and discovered a split lower lip. Try as I might, I could not get her to stop talking and tell me what had happened.

Finally I could take no more. With one jolt of frustration and with what little arm strength I possessed, I picked her up and laid her back on her bed. I was a little abrupt, and she yelled, "Ouch, you hurt me!"

Now at least I had her attention—or so I thought.

I looked her over and saw that her right elbow was expanded to twice its normal size. Kathleen had arrived by then and we applied an ice pack to the damaged elbow. Mom had calmed down but had no recollection of how she got out of her bed and on to the floor or hurt her elbow. I was hoping our little act of first aid would be sufficient for the injury. Kathleen and I cleaned Mom, keeping the ice on her elbow, hoping the swelling would go down. All it did was give Mom another reason to complain because she felt we were both trying to make her cold.

My daughter and I discussed a few courses of action, including my thought that we see how the elbow looks in the morning. Kathleen gave me this look of consternation I knew too well that meant, "Dad, open your eyes and get her to the emergency room."

I really wanted to prevent the inevitable trip to the emergency room. This was not a matter of the injury alone. This was turning my dementia-afflicted mother loose on an emergency room clientele where she was apt to, and would, say anything on her mind. I concurred it was the only course of action.

As I placed her in the car and strapped her in the seat next to me for the ride to the hospital, my candid, selfish thoughts were of the long evening I would spend in the emergency room. Once surrounded by people, my mother could turn into a living reincarnation of Belle Barth (a bawdy lounge comedian of the 1950s).

As I drove, I asked Mom (in the vain hope that she could understand me) to please refrain from any racial or sexual questions, as some people might be offended. Even though in pain, Mom told me that no one expects her to be perfect all the time and that I should be understanding since I am far from perfect as well. I figured here it comes again, another reference to the homely son, Stevie.

Pulling up to the curb of the emergency room I got out and grabbed a wheelchair. Being as careful as I could not to hurt her, I maneuvered her into the wheelchair. If her elbow hurt, she wasn't complaining about it, so my hopes were that this was just a bruise.

Entering the ER, my worst hopes were realized as the place was full of people of all ages and races, with no empty corner to sit with Mom away from her roving eye.

One thing about Mom's dementia: no matter who she saw with her eyes, it would translate to a different person by the time it got to her brain, and then manifest with her mouth providing an unpredictable narrative. Once during a visit to an endocrinologist, she was seated next to a woman with a patch over her left eye. After sitting quietly for a few moments, Mom turned to the woman and asked, "Hilda, when did you lose your good eye?"

Back in the ER, I rolled her over to the registration desk, where two receptionists were checking in patients. The elderly looking gentleman receptionist at the desk asked the usual, "How can I help you?"

I responded, "This is my mother, and she has injured her elbow in a fall."

My mother took instant exception with my answering the receptionist's question. Barking at me loudly she screamed, *"I can talk for myself! I don't need your help!"*

Mother took over. The gentleman receptionist was now about to become a player in one of the most bizarre events along the dementia highway.

The receptionist smilingly asked Mom, "Would you like to sit over there [motioning to the crowded emergency room] and complete the information form?"

Mother, showing the brash arrogance that was never part of her personality before dementia, leaned forward and clearly stated, "No, I want *you* to ask me all the questions on the form, one by one, and I will give you the answers."

That receptionist could not have been kinder or more understanding as he asked every question.

The Q and A between Mom, the receptionist, and me went like this.

> "Name?"
>
> Mother responded, "What wants to know?"
>
> I tried to help, "Mom, please tell the gentleman your name."
>
> With a nasty Bertha glare at me, "Shut up ... don't need your help."
>
> The receptionist sensing some tension responded, "It's okay. So what's your name?"
>
> Mom looked at me. "Well? Tell the man."
>
> As I rolled my eyes skyward, I responded, "Bertha Hoag."
>
> Mom snapped, "*Stupid*! That's not your name, that's *my* name." She turned to the receptionist. "He always makes this hard. You should see his handsome brother."
>
> Starting to figure out that Mom isn't all there, he said, ""Bertha? What's your name?"
>
> "Oh? Have we met? My name is Bertha Hoag, but you can call me Bokie."
>
> He looked at me. "Do you want to answer these questions? It will go faster?"
>
> Mother was weaving this conversation with her dementia flags flying. "I can answer for myself. Young man, you ask me every question and you"— she looked at me—"just keep your mouth closed."
>
> "Bertha, what is your date of birth?"
>
> "A girl never tells."
>
> The receptionist's next question: "Your address?"
>
> "It's 164 Myrtle Avenue, Fitchburg, Massachusetts."
>
> I stood behind Mom, shaking my head no. This was her address in high school.
>
> "Bertha ... if you have a driver's license, I might do this faster."
>
> "I don't drive. What's your friggin' rush? You got a date?"

The Patience Meter is reaching red alert, so I called out, "It's 11 Woodland Drive, Wallingford."

"That's where Tommy lives." She added, "I am doing a good job of answering. I don't need your help. You ask all the questions on the form to me. Okay?"

He responded, "Okay."

Now I've committed to silence. I have her insurance cards in my hands and am ready to give them to the receptionist, but that's it.

"Person to contact in case of emergency or next of kin?"

"My sister Florence."

Fanny has been dead for more than twenty-five years.

"Occupation?"

Mom responded, "Call girl."

"Now, you don't work, do you, Bertha?"

"Yes I do ... call girl. What's wrong with that?"

The receptionist was having a blast doing this interview with Mom, and since he was smiling and Mom was feeling her "oats," I let it go.

The interview was finally complete, and the insurance cards were copied by the receptionist. With that, we returned to the holding room and waited to be called. I moved Mom's wheelchair to the most remote part of the room with a sigh of relief that the first part of our emergency room visit was over.

Due to Mom's age they called her almost right away to enter the examination room. Mom was wonderfully quiet, probably a little worn out from her interview.

A doctor came right over to see my mother. This was the fastest service I had ever experienced in an ER. Thank God! The doctor was bending over my mother looking at her elbow, which was still badly swollen. His stethoscope hung around his neck.

I was sitting behind Mom and saw her grab the bottom of the stethoscope, and without warning she yelled into it, "It's Bokie."

The doctor flinched, looked at Mom, and said, "Oh, I've heard about you."

Recalling that moment, I wondered how he or anyone could have said he'd heard about Mom. I wrote it off as just one of those things doctors say when they have a difficult patient. I was soon to discover what the doctor meant.

After his brief examination, he ordered X-rays, and shortly thereafter, I was left sitting alone in the little cubicle where Mom was examined. Writing in my chronicle that I always carried with me and wrote in daily, I recollected the back and forth between the receptionist and Mom, still unable to find the humor in it all.

A nurse came around, sticking her head into the room with this broad smile, and asked how I was doing. The way she asked seemed a little strange, with this little giggle at the end of her enquiry. A few minutes later a young male intern with the same nurse ducked their heads in and looked around the cubicle.

I asked, "Can I help you?"

The nurse, in a rather timid manner, responded, "Where did the little old woman go who was in here?"

Starting to get the feeling that there was something I don't know and should know about, I said, "Mom is getting an X-ray and should be back shortly. Is everything all right?"

The young intern almost glared at me and asked, "Is that your mother?"

I smiled and restated, "Yes, she is my mother. Is there something wrong here?"

The nurse quickly apologized for intruding, adding, "Sir, don't take this the wrong way. We just heard that this old lady was saying she is a call girl."

Not wishing to appear offended by any of this, I tried to defuse the moment. I explained that Mother was just trying to be funny when she talked to the receptionist. They turned to leave as another nurse met them at the edge of the doorway and asked them, "Is this the room with the ninety-year-old prostitute?"

Obviously word had spread across the emergency room staff. Thank you, Alzheimer's!

I waited for about thirty minutes and Mom was brought back to the little examination cubicle wide awake and telling the aide who was pushing her gurney that she was hungry. I was glad to see her hungry and was anxious to hear the results of the X-ray. I brought Mom a cup of cold water that she asked for, and before she took a sip, she asked me to sing a song for her.

Finally, I thought, the delusion of the moment was finally at an end. I asked her what song she wanted me to sing, and she requested one she had taught me long ago. It was a Billy Holiday tune, "God Bless the Child."

I was happy to sing it to her if for no other reason because this "call girl" thing was surely over and she recognized me as her son again. Guess again, Stephen!

After a long wait, an old friend, Dr. B., whom I knew from my years of football coaching and the doctor who took care of my daughter Maureen's broken wrist came into the room with a broad smile that he always possessed. It was so good to see him and have him make the diagnosis of my mom's elbow.

I wasted no time and asked about her elbow. He was talking only to me and Mom didn't care, so everything had returned to normal ... or so I thought.

The doctor told me Mom had broken her elbow and would require immediate surgery that he would perform right away. At least she was in the best hands possible, the incredible Dr. B. He explained the procedure and the approximate recovery time, and I was resolved to sit out the surgery at the hospital, which would be a few more hours.

Now, Dr. B. was the best of surgeons, but an even better man. He could make you laugh but always got down to business when it came to the health of a patient.

He went over to my mother's bed and asked quietly, "How are you, Bertha?"

Mom didn't answer. She just looked at him.

Dr. B. attempted again. "So, Bertha, I hear you're a call girl."

My eyes almost popped out of my head in astonishment over the question and I was at a loss to utter a sound, but Mom chimed right back at him, "Yes, it's a living."

Dr. B. kept the chat alive. "Well, Bertha ... Are you active?"

Mom's causal response? "No, I just lay there."

Son's Rule: It is easy to get embarrassed over a parent who is suffering from Alzheimer's/dementia if you let yourself measure your mom or dad by the standards you have come to know him or her by prior to this disease. Remember that embarrassment, that feeling of awkwardness and self-consciousness, is what *you* feel, not what your mom (or dad) currently feels due to dementia. When and if you find humor in what they do, don't forget you are not laughing at them but using the mechanism God has given you to deal with the pain you feel for a parent you love who cannot stop the impact of the disease. And neither can you.

Chapter 16

A Date with Ralphie

During 2008 there was an increase in the number of hallucinations that started after seven thirty, Mom's bedtime. Aside from the concern that she might extradite herself from her bed that was security barred, there was my concern for the toll her machinations were having on Tommy.

As I have stated, Mom and Tom were close-knit throughout his lifetime. They had always lived in the same home, and Mom was his confidant, his protector, his teacher, and his best friend. Tommy's day-to-day observation of Mom's gradual deterioration due to dementia might have been a blessing for him. If Mom's condition had changed quickly, I know he could not have handled it given the fragility of his emotional status.

Tommy was used to quiet evenings at home, watching television, petting Sherbie, the cat, or playing a video game or two. Serene was how most of Tommy's life was spent at home. I'm sure that became the norm, especially after I went off to college. Now, with Mom beset with the fantasies and delusions of dementia, the evenings were anything but calm.

Once the sun went down, Mom would "see" almost anything. These visions included her boisterous participation into an endless array of scenarios. Her uncontrollable shouting and talking to mysterious people was more than Tommy could deal with mentally and physically. It got to the point in 2008 where I almost relented, beginning in earnest to locate a nursing home where Mom would be in a quality environment for Alzheimer's suffers for the rest of her life.

It was hurtful enough for me and our entire family to see what Mom was becoming, but now it was affecting Tommy, and that was one too many fronts to fight successfully.

I began to spend more time in the later evenings with her in her bedroom. I would sit at the edge of her bed talking to her and hoping she would respond. If she asked me to sing, I would follow up by asking her what song she wanted. One of the blessings of those evenings sitting with her was that she never asked me to sing a song I did not know. When I sang, she often sang a phrase with me and that made me smile, because it showed her memory was still in play. One of the songs we sang together in *responsive style* was, "I Got It Bad, and That Ain't Good," an Ella Fitzgerald song. Mom loved Ella. Whenever I think of the lyrics, I still get tears in my eyes because Mom must have asked me a hundred times to sing it for her. I can hear the words now: "Never treats me sweet and gentle, the way he should, I got it bad and that ain't good." I miss singing to her.

My best hope was that I would just watch her sleep. On the other hand, if Mom broke out into one of those participatory hallucinations, I tried to contain the chatter, although I didn't have a clue how I was going to do it from one day to the next. God was in tune with my heart, and by His grace alone I was brought into the most unbelievable manifestations of theatrical improvisation never before imagined.

Hence, as mother began talking, yelling, or interacting with a fantasy person, I tried my best to become that person. It is important to remember that when Mom was experiencing these visions as a result of Alzheimer's/dementia, she was wide awake.

The room might have been dark with the lights out except for a small night light, but in her thoughts it might have been the lavishly lit Norumbega Park in Boston during the World War II era. Mom had often described Norumbega, Whalom Park, and a number of other locations where she and her friends would listen and dance to the big bands in the 1940s.

One of the most amazing aspects of her dementia was how she could cross-stitch together little snippets of her fading memory with real people (like me) she was actually seeing with her own eyes, resulting in one melodramatic delusion after another.

Mom had graduated from Fitchburg High School in Massachusetts in 1934. As a young boy, Mother would talk to me about her high school, her favorite teachers, and a few of her best girlfriends, but she never mentioned any young men from her school days. I never thought much about it. Actually I never gave it a second thought. That is until she fanaticized or relived some rather provocative moments with some "lads" from Fitchburg, adding to the "spice rack" of dementia.

The event I now relate, although somewhat awkward to have gone through, provided me with yet another tiny corner of understanding as to what my mother might really have been like as a teenager in the 1930s.

One evening, I arrived after Chelsea, Mom's loving caregiver had put Mom to bed. It was after eight and I was dragging.

As I came in the side door, Tommy yelled out, "She's at it again. Mom is driving me crazy. Why don't you put her in a nursing home, Stevie?"

Tommy must have been on the edge of losing it if he was talking about putting his mother in a home, so up to her room I went.

I heard Mom's voice as I entered the darkened room and turned on the light on her dressing table. She was wide-eyed awake and having a gesture-filled conversation with someone.

I decided to begin with a *practical* approach. I went to her bedside and tried to communicate in a normal manner. "Mom ... Mom ... it's me, Stevie." How many times would I have to learn that when dealing with Mother during this time of dementia, "pragmatic and logical" approaches to Mom's fantasies were like eating pasta through a straw.

Mom looked right at me, and I looked right into her eyes, but she wasn't seeing her son, Stevie.

Mother, yelled out, "Fannie [her late favorite older sister] ... Fannie ... Fan are you there?"

I didn't say a word yet. I wanted to see where this was going.

"Fan," my mother continued, "I got the audition. Will Dora let me wear her blue dress?"

I figured now was a good time to try to get Mom quiet since she was getting loud and I could hear Tommy downstairs talking to himself, saying he was going to call 911 if she didn't shut up.

Rather than call her "Mom" again, I increased my voice level to try to get her attention with the use of her nickname. "Bokie, how are you?"

I wasn't expecting her to answer. I just wanted to get her out of this hallucination. With a moment of hesitation, mom answered me. "*Ralphie, you're early.*"

I was thinking, *Does she really believe I'm some guy name Ralphie?* I determined that playing along was the best course of action.

The conversation continued.

"Ralphie, where are we going tonight?"

"Where do you want to go?"

"Shhh, you're talking too loud; Fanny will hear us."

I was wondering if it was possible to interact with her fantasy of the moment by playing a role. The way she was looking at me, she might actually believe I was this Ralphie. I decided to engage in my best improvisation.

Mom said, "Do you think we should?"

This was dangerous. What did Mom think she and Ralphie should do or not do? I decided to stay in character. "Bokie, perhaps we should stay home."

"Ralphie ... don't start that now."

Start what? This would have been interesting, if it wasn't my own mother. Yuck!

"Ralphie, Ralphie ... don't be so fresh."

Up to this point, all Mom was doing besides engaging in this conversation was staring at me. Then with the suddenness that is characteristic of dementia, mom said, "Ralphie, give me one more." She pointed to her lips and closed her eyes.

Does she really think I'm Ralphie? I decided to stay quiet for a while and see where her illusion was going.

"Fan, we're leaving. We are going to the boulder to meet the kids."

I remained quiet for approximately fifteen minutes. I hoped Mom would close her eyes and fall asleep so I could get home and have dinner.

Son's Rule: As we sift through the memories and memorabilia of our parents, be a bit cautious. You never know what you might find or uncover. During my walk with Mom during those years of Alzheimer's, I was never quite sure what was real or unreal. This I do know: Mom had a lot more fun as a young girl than I ever let myself dare to imagine.

Chapter 17

No Giving Up

The scope and progressive nature of Alzheimer's/dementia took Mom and me through some rough times. Of the most challenging was the final stage of the disease because I could not give up in the face of what was becoming inevitable. Mom's mental facilities had all but left her, and her body, muscles, and bones were all too thin to withstand many more days. I saw it unfold. I even said to my loving colleagues at work, "I'm losing her," but I refused to believe it. I just couldn't believe her time on earth—with me—was almost at an end. It all went against the grain to work that hard, that long, only to lose her.

There was no denying that caring for her during this final stage was more intensive and emotionally draining because she no longer recognized me at all. Even the momentary recognition of me of past months was almost gone.

A Brief Chat with Mom

Our once playful, sarcastic, sometimes caustic but always loving discourse had become a one-way conversation. Even after all of the years facing Alzheimer's/dementia together, my frustration was showing now, more than ever. I could not let her go not knowing me.

In the fall of 2012, I sat with Mom and had a "chat" with her—but with me speaking both parts. Mom could no longer say more than a few words.

I had conversations with her with me speaking the part of whomever she believed was in the room. I played the parts of her sister Fannie; her father, "Paaaaa"; boyfriend Ralphie; and anyone else who flashed across Mom's dementia screen.

On November 16, 2012, I sat on the edge of her bed. I was close enough to her face to almost place my head on her pillow with her. Her light-blue eyes peered into mine. I wanted to talk with my mother. I wanted her to talk with me. I had become a number of different people for her, speaking for those many dead and imagined individuals.

This night, in the midst of frustration and denial, I had a conversation with Mother, and I spoke for Mom.

The conversation went just this way.

Me: "Mom, you look great tonight."

Me (for Mom): "Thank you, Stevie. You look good yourself."

Me: "So what would you like for Christmas this year?"

Me (for Mom): "Oh, you know me. I don't want a lot, a fur, a string of pearls." A pause, and then, "Stevie, what do you want for Christmas?"

I started to well up and cry, really cry. "Mom, I want you back. I want you to be you again."

Diagnosis without Words

By Christmas week, which was Mom's birthday week (December 23), I had to get her to her doctor earlier than her regularly scheduled appointment. Mom was constantly falling asleep and had a hard time holding her head up. I thought a shot of vitamin B or some other drug would put some energy into the old girl and she would regain some of her vigor. I was staying in prayer and would not harbor a defeatist thought during this time. Chelsea, our superstar homecare worker, was doing everything in her power to keep Mom active and awake, but I saw it in Chelsea's eyes that Mom was slipping on us. I believe Chelsea could see how I would not give in to the signs of the end time, but she never said a word about Mom dying or hinted that the end was near.

I took my mother to see her doctor, an incredible gentleman, Dr. Richard Wein who appreciated Mother's wit and dancing spirit. It was just after Christmas, and it was a physical struggle to get Mom to put one leg in front of the other. Mom could no longer use the walker because she did not have the strength in her arms and legs to hold herself up. This meant I had to wrap my arms around her and walk her as if my legs were hers.

Once we arrived on Fair Street and parked in front of the doctor's office, I really struggled to lift her from the car to a position where I could wrap my arms about her waist and walk her to the door. Propping the door open to the office with my hip, and with the help of the doctor's nurse, I got her to the couch in the center of the waiting room. I kept Mom under my arm, and her head kept dropping on my shoulder, falling asleep.

I would shake her a little and call her to wake up. I sang quietly to her without her solicitation, making believe she had asked me sing.

The nurse brought her a wheelchair, and I pushed it into the doctor's examining room. Each of the nurses came in to say hello to Mom, and that touched my heart. I just couldn't keep her awake.

The good doctor came in, sat across from us, and looked at Mom. He asked how she was doing, and that was my cue to say she needed a shot of something to increase her energy and keep her awake. The doctor tried to communicate with her, but she was unresponsive. I asked again about a vitamin B shot or anything that would help.

I looked at this doctor, whom I had grown to greatly admire, and swallowed hard to avoid the knot that was building in my throat. I looked right into his eyes, and for a few moments he did not speak, but he gave me the diagnosis in his silence.

He said, "Look, let's get a blood test on her and see what we might do."

I was grasping at any straw at this point. The doctor told me to take her across the street to a clinical laboratory for the blood test.

Getting a helping hand from the nurse back to my car, I put Mom back in the front seat, begging her to stay awake. The distance from the doctor's office to the lab was no more than fifty yards away, but I had to drive her as the wheelchair belonged to the doctor's office. She was unable to walk and just would not stay awake for me.

I pulled up over the curb and almost up the ramp to the back door. Mom would not, or was unable to help me at all in getting her out of the car. I took her in my arms with her head on my shoulder. I didn't know if I could carry her to the door. She was only eighty or so pounds, but I am a smaller man who never had anything akin to arm strength.

I called out to a passerby and one person coming out the door, asking them to assist me to the building, but no one would come to my aid. Here I was with my mother, who was now asleep, in my arms, and I had no idea how I was going to open the door to the building to get her a blood test.

By the grace of God, an elderly gentleman driving past the building saw me at the door carrying Mom in my arms as if she was a young child. He stopped his car, got out, and opened the front door for us. If I wasn't carrying my mom I would have kissed him.

Once inside, I kicked at the door to the lab to get someone to open it, but no one answered. Mom was getting heavy. I was asking God to strengthen me, support me, and help me. Finally, another person entering the lab for a test opened the door for us.

I carefully placed Mom in the first chair I saw. I looked over at the windowed desk at a lab technician who registers clients for testing and wondered why she couldn't have opened the door for us.

Making eye contact, she said, "You will have sign in here."

I couldn't leave Mom as she would have fallen out of her chair.

I asked the technician to please bring the form for me to sign. I could not leave my mom.

The technician finally stood up, looked down at us, and, seeing mom bent over in the chair with me kneeling in front of it, Mom's head against my chest, callously asked, "Is she alive?"

If I wasn't almost physically and emotionally spent, I think I might have reacted most angrily. I assured her my mother was alive and we needed a blood test.

One other person in the waiting room heard that terrible question and shook his head in disgust. I carried Mother to the room for the test that lasted but a few minutes.

Now the task was to get mother back to the car and home. The gentleman who was in the waiting room was gracious enough to hold all the doors open as I carried Mother in my arms back to the car.

All the way back to the house I kept looking over at my sleeping mother with tears in my eyes as I drove. More than once I yelled out, "Don't you die on me, Mom."

The doctor told me the prognosis with his smile and eyes. He didn't really say a word that needed to be said. My eyes and ears weren't working, but my heart was, and it heard what the doctor wanted me to know. For the first time, I knew the time was close at hand.

Son's Rule: No two people react the same to impending death. For those of us who share the decline of our mom's or dad's mind and body to Alzheimer's/dementia, we may deny what our senses see and hear because of all Mom or Dad were just a few years ago. Our parents cannot ask for our love or help because of the dementia. This is why we each need to give our greatest acts of love to them.

The blend of love we give Mom or Dad may block our senses, allowing us to serve him or her without limits, but when God speaks to your heart, we will know the time of passing is at hand.

Chapter 18

The "I Love You" Moment

As a typical child of the 1950s, or any decade for that matter, I saw the toys and things other children had on our street and wanted them. Our next door neighbor, George, had a red Schwinn bike and I wanted one. Ricky, from down the street, had a Don Larsen baseball glove and I wanted one. There are always those elements of envy and want in young children. I was no different.

I don't remember ever wanting one toy that "I gotta have," but there was something that stayed with me as a "want" from my early childhood to adulthood.

I wanted, just once, to hear my mother or father say "I love you" to me. It may seem odd to most people since everyone says "I love you." I say it to my wife and my grown daughters every time I see or talk to them, but for my mom and dad, those three words were never uttered to me as a child.

Growing up on a little street in Wallingford, Connecticut, I would hear the fathers and mothers of my friends say those words to them. When I was eight or nine years old it started to confuse me. What did "I love you" mean to those other people? I never heard Mom and Dad say it to each other, and they sure didn't say it to Tom and me.

You must understand I lived in a home with a volatile father who demanded strict adherence to his rules and commands. Dad would often evoke a preface to his limited conversation with us that started, "When I was in the service ..."

Whatever followed those words were as important as ordering a charge on a beach head. This meant that he expected Mom, Tommy, and me to jump to whatever order he gave, and we did. When Dad came home from work and we were in the house, we knew to scoot to our bedroom and not to make a sound until he called us for dinner.

Occasionally Dad would throw the baseball or football with me, but we did not speak to each other during this activity. He would show me how run back on a fly ball or catch a pass over my head, but he desired no discourse from me. When Dad was laid off from his factory for periods of time, we might go days without any conversation in the house. Dad's rule was absolute: "Don't speak unless you are spoken to."

When Dad wasn't home it was a whole different story. Mom would sometimes have the neighborhood teenagers girls over the house, listening to music and dancing. Mom loved the energy of the teenagers, especially as the Rock and Roll era was unfolding in the 1950s. Mom would engage me in all of this, asking me to sing and dance for the teenage girls. I think if I was a few years older I would have enjoyed that a lot more. One of the things I remember is how the girls would all leave before Dad was scheduled to arrive from work. They would hug Mom and say things like, "Thank you, Bokie," or "Love you, Bokie."

Those words, "love you," did not escape my ears. I could talk to Mom about anything when Dad wasn't home, so I asked her what "I love you" meant. Mom would say something like, "Oh, that means someone is happy."

I knew that was not the full truth because Mom would cut the conversation short. She never was short with explanations about anything else. The more she avoided discussing "I love you," the more interested I became.

I asked friends what "I love you" means. The guys always looked at me strangely or just laughed. Granted we were all eight, nine, or ten years old, but I wanted to know. After a field trip with my fifth-grade class, I ended up seated next to my teacher on the bus ride back to the school. With little to say to a teacher, I remember asking her, "What does 'I love you' mean?" She smiled and told me to go ask my mother. I felt like a jerk, but it wouldn't be the last time.

Looking back, I know Tommy and I were loved by our parents, but it was a continuing puzzlement. When I was eleven (and I remember because that was the week Dad was going to take me to see my first Yankee game, although he decided not to go that morning), I had an opportunity to talk with Mom about the phrase.

In one of those moments I remember rather vividly but can't recall how it came up in conversation, Mom and I were walking to downtown Wallingford to pay bills. Mom never learned to drive, so she walked everywhere, and I loved walking with her. I asked her to explain why we (in our family) don't say "I love you."

She told me, "We don't have to say it."

I brought up the argument that other people say it, and they say it on television. Finally, the answer came forth. Mother explained, "Your father does not want any of us to say those words." I must have kept at the topic too long, because Mom got a little mad at me and sped up her walking and didn't say much to me the rest of the way.

That would be the last time this topic was ever brought up by me.

As love entered my life with relationships, I began using those three words and made a pledge that when I had children of my own, I would shower them with "I love yous," and I did and have. In my walk with Jesus I learned a whole new appreciation for God's gift of love. I find loving others and telling them I love them as easy as anything I have ever done.

Sitting by my father's bed in the hospital during the last few days of his life, I told him I loved him. The last words I said to him as he died in my arms were, "I love you." That meant a lot to me, and although he was not conscious, I hope it meant something to him.

When Mom's care became my principle responsibility in 2002, I committed to surrounding her with my love. I inserted "I love you" into my everyday vocabulary with Mom, no matter how she rolled her eyes or ignored it. Even after Dad's death she maintained the "no saying 'I love you' edict." However, every day, every good-bye from me, every phone conversation with me included "I love you, Mom." It may not have had much value to her after so many years of the moratorium, but it meant a lot to me.

In the ten years of the escalading erosion of Mom's mental and physical health, very so often, especially at Mom's bedtime, I would put my face close to hers and whisper, "Mom ... tell me you love me."

The last years with Mom gave me ample opportunities to say "I love you," making up for all my bedtimes as a child when the phrase was forbidden.

I thought with the unpredictable moods and emotions of my mother with Alzheimer's/Dementia, I might elicit an "I love you" at least once as her life wound down. How I just once wanted her to tell me she loved me. It may sound silly after so many years, but it was important.

The Moment

It was a Thursday (January 5, 2012), and that meant getting the food order at Stop & Shop. As I had for more than ten years, I went to see Mom, asking her and Tommy if there was anything they wanted beyond the normal list of items.

Mom hadn't recognized me in a few years by this time, but I kept up the routine as my own little rebellion against Alzheimer's/dementia. We who serve parents with this disease are pretty resolute, and each of us holds out some degree of hope that this affliction can be turned around, if not cured, if we love our parents a little more each day.

I went to Mom's beside with paper and pen in hand, asking her if there was something special she would like me to purchase. Mom didn't answer, and given the events of the last week at the medical diagnostic lab and with Dr. Wein and his staff, I felt sick inside that I might not have but a few more months with her. Mom said nothing to me. I kissed her on the cheek and told her "I love you" and went off to do the shopping with my list and the one Tommy wrote.

As I walked the aisles of Stop & Shop, I chanced to recall the places where I sang to mother. I was rather emotional that day. I didn't know why. I ran into people I knew or those who knew me. For some reason, this Thursday of shopping felt different. I was moving rapidly down the aisles, knowing where every item was since I had done this for more than ten years, fifty-two weeks a year. I believe I could do most of the shopping blindfolded if I had to.

I was almost done when I ran into an old friend, a wonderful woman who I knew in high school. We exchanged greetings and had a short conversation. She enquired about Mom as I was turning to go. I looked back at her. My smile was replaced by a lump in my throat, almost succumbing to tears, saying the words, "I'm going to lose her."

Whatever overwhelmed me so instantly, I knew I must return to my Mom's bedside quickly.

Pulling up under the carport at Mom's house on that cold January night, I moved the groceries from my backseat to the kitchen table, and Tommy began to put them away. I was anxious to get upstairs and see Mom and dispel this feeling of dread. After all these years with her, now I was acting like a big baby.

Entering her room, I turned on her night table lamp. Chelsea (Mom's loving care worker) had completed bathing and dressing Mom for bed. Mom, wearing a red and white flannel nightgown, was almost asleep and propped up against her pillow.

I went to the left side of her bed, kneeling on the floor so I could get my face close to hers. I told her I just finished getting the weekly food order, but she did not respond. I waited a few minutes and began to talk again, asking what she'd had for dinner. Even at that late stage of Alzheimer's/dementia, I kept trying to keep her short-term and long-term memory working.

Mom finally looked over at me. My face was maybe six inches from hers. I spoke softly to her even if she could not or would not speak to me. Mom's blue eyes bore right into mine.

Finally, she said one word in the smallest of voices: "Sing."

That little word that she had spoken to me a thousand times before now brought me to the brink of tears. I bit down on the side of my tongue, now wanting to cry. With all my heart, I whispered to God, "Help me."

"What do you want me to sing?" I whispered.

Mom did not answer. After a few seconds she said it again: "Sing."

I had to sing boldly. I had to sing loud. I had to sing to an imaginary audience of hundreds or I could not sing at all. If I had tried to sing softly, I would have been reduced to tears.

I thought quickly of a song she loved me to sing, one she'd taught when I was very young after taking me to see Stubby Kay perform it in *Guys and Dolls*. I got up off my knees and positioned myself at the foot of the bed. I stood tall and raised my hands as she taught me. There, just as she instructed me in 1957 or '58, I performed it for her. "Last night I dreamed I got on the boat to heaven, and by some chance I had brought my dice along ..."

I was good that night. Mom always told me I would not need an audience to tell me if I put on a good performance. My heart would tell me.

When I finished, her eyes were closed and she was asleep. I kissed her good night, told her I loved her, and turned off the light. I closed her door and walked down the four stairs to the kitchen and left the house for my car. As I stood by my car on this cold winter night, I felt I could not leave. Not yet anyway.

Walking back upstairs, I reentered her room and turned on the light. Mom didn't notice me or the light. I returned to my kneeling position at her bedside and put my face right in front of hers, so close that I could see a little flicker of her eye lips.

"Mom, Mom ... Mom," I said above my normal voice. I wanted her awake so much right now.

She opened her eyes and looked at me.

"Mom, tell me you love me," I said. *"Mom, tell me you love, please,"* I begged. Holding back tears, I tried again, *"Say I love you."*

Looking right into my eyes, Mom softly said three words: "I love you."

I knew it was time. God was calling because God gave me my heart's desire.

My mom, Bertha Hoag, died the next day, January 6, 2012.

Son's Rule: As the son or daughter of a parent with Alzheimer's/dementia, you are paying an emotional price. With a mom or dad who at some point will not be able respond to you, *your* heart will have to be the voice of your parent. You will need to listen to your heart to hear your mom or dad. Never let what he or she has become because of this disease diminish the best of what your mom or dad was, and still is, to you.

Author's Note

It feels as though Mom only died the other day. The imprint of the years we shared as she took the descending staircase of dementia is forever etched in my thoughts. In writing this book I have gleaned the essence of meaningful lyric and lesson so that others might walk down those stairs with their beloved parent, family member, or patient in the knowledge that it is not all pain and ugliness.

In loving someone so much that we choose to share the most difficult years, we must never fail to celebrate the fullness of his or her life. We as loving children and caregivers are strengthened for every minute we give of ourselves to them. Each moment we seek the best of ourselves to meet their temporal need, we galvanize our own lives.

May God bless you in all ways,
Stephen W. Hoag

About the Author

Photo by Tim Gannon

Stephen W. Hoag was raised in Wallingford, Connecticut. An innovative and passionate educator, Dr. Hoag has been a member of the State Department of Education for over 35 years. An accomplished speaker, he has entertained and thrilled audiences throughout his lifetime with his anecdotes and philosophy on teaching, athletic coaching, parenthood and leadership. Dr. Hoag has received recognition for teaching, coaching, education assessment and community service. Of note, he was the recipient of the national 2008 C. Thomas Olivo Award, given to one person each year for leadership and creativity in student assessment by the National Occupational Competency Testing Institute. Dr. Hoag leads the ground-breaking Developing Tomorrow's Professionals program for Black and Hispanic Young Men.

CPSIA information can be obtained at www.ICGtesting.com
Printed in the USA
BVOW04s0037240114

342848BV00001B/92/P